DAY BY
DAY

poetry **Pt** *today*

DAY BY
DAY

Edited by
Claire Evans

First published in Great Britain in 1997 by Poetry Today, an imprint of Penhaligon Page Ltd, Upper Dee Mill, Llangollen, Wales.

© Copyright Contributors 1997

A Catalogue record for this book is available from the British Library.

ISBN 1862260117

Typesetting and layout, Penhaligon Page Ltd, Wales.
Printed and bound by Forward Press Ltd, England

*'Avoid enquiring into what will be tomorrow,
and count as gain each day that fortune
grants you'*

(Horace [Odes, I, 11 Line1])

Series Introduction

The Poetry Today series of anthologies was launched to provide a substantial showcase for today's poets. A permanent record of perception, concern and creativity in our late twentieth century lives.

Poetry is a coat of many colours. Today's poets write in a limitless array of styles: traditional rhyming poetry is as alive and kicking today as modern free-verse. Language ranges from easily accessible to intricate and elusive.

Poems have a lot to offer in our fast-paced 'instant' world. Reading poems gives us an opportunity to sit back and explore ourselves and the world around us.

Today's poetry readers have as varied tastes as the poets who write for them. The poems in this volume complement each other and provide insight into the real life of a society heading for the third millennium.

Foreword

Day by Day is the first anthology in this series
of themed books. *Day by Day* represents our
thoughts on life in today's ever-changing
world. The poems cover issues that affect us all
day by day. There are moments which create
laughter, tears and sighs.

This compilation provides ample food for
thought. The poets bring a wealth of experience
and insight to their work. No aspect of life is
missed, no point of view left out. I hope that
you enjoy these lines on life as much as I did.

Contents

The Poems

DIY

Notes

I am 76, happily married, have four lovely daughters, seven grandchildren and one great-grandson. I live in sheltered housing in Sompting, a Sussex village, 'twixt downs and sea.

I started writing poetry, when myeloma was diagnosed two years ago, it is terminal, but I am responding well to treatment.

I have won an Editor's Choice Award for one poem.

I enjoy reading, knitting, writing letters and poetry. I swim, weather permitting.

Nothing inspires me to write, the poems just 'come'.

Do you think you've got it right?
That shade of red is much too bright,
Are those your brushes on the stair?
You really must not leave them there,
Why is this bucket in the sink?
No, I do not like that shade of pink,
For the bathroom do you say?
Oh dear, this is a dreadful day
Why can't we get into the loo?
Because you're painting it turquoise blue!
Look out, that paper on the wall,
Is not going on straight at all.
You've kicked that bucket, now the paste,
Is slopping over and going to waste.
Lumps of putty everywhere,
You've even got some in your hair,
And what's this splodge upon the door?
And sticky footprints on the floor?
Before I go into the loony-bin,
Please, let's call the experts in!

Helen Hazlerigg

Notes

I am 45 years old and I have been married for 24 years now. My husband, Geoffrey, has taken care of me for the past twenty years because I am disabled and, therefore, I have to rely on him for nearly all my basic needs to help me lead as normal a life as possible.

We haven't any children and we live in the country, between Ivybridge and Ermington in South Devon.

We share a hobby in photography.

Last year I tried to write a poem for each member of my family for my own pleasure. I found it so enjoyable that I thought I would try to write one for my husband in order to thank him for taking care of me over the past years. This time I decided to see if a company would accept it for publication and I was most pleasantly surprised when they did.

I only had a secondary school education and I was a slow learner, so my main drawback was, (and still is), my grammar and punctuation etc. Still, in spite of this, since then I have had a few of my poems published in anthologies.

The Robin

As I sit beside my window
Let me tell you what I see
When I look out on our garden
I can see the flowers and trees
A robin sits among them
And although it's hard to see
I hear the robin calling
As if he's calling me
But when I look much closer
I also see some bees
That really seem so busy
As they buzz from tree to tree
If only you could see them too
I know you would agree
How nice it is to watch them
And thank God that you can see

Merilyn Gulley

Deserted

She lives alone with her memories clear,
She lives alone and none can hear,

Her gentle sobs as she lonely cries,
As she breaks her nails when 'ere she tries,

To do the tasks that a man should do,
To hammer a nail or turn a screw.

To paint the hall and paint the stairs,
And struggle through her numerous cares.

To walk the dog and feed the cat,
And once in a while to have a chat,

With a neighbour or two, in the street,
When luck perchance would have them meet.

She'd like to stay and talk all day,
But the neighbours soon are on their way.

Do they know the curse of loneliness?
When a loved one's gone, and happiness,

Left so quick, on that fateful day,
And sadness came in the house to stay.

And now she lives and sleeps alone,
With no man at her side to call her own,

No man to love her through the night,
No man to shield her from life's fight.

Now she struggles alone from day to day,
With a paupers purse her bills to pay.

Those bills which arrive with alarming speed,
Should she pay them now, or will she need?

That money to pay for urgent repairs,
She wished to God, she could shed these cares.

But each month she manages to survive,
And she, the dog and cat are alive.

But it's only just living, and surely no fun,
For a woman whose left for another one.

J E Terry

The Local Rag

Notes

My name is Hilda Costello, I was born in Oldham, Lancashire in 1931. The principle industry was cotton spinning and at that time it was booming.

I was married in 1963 and my daughter, Theresa, was born the year after.

The birth of my daughter inspired me to write poetry which takes me into another world where I am able to forget my troubles.

I've read the paper
From the front page,
To the back.
A child has been born,
It's someone's birthday,
Someone is celebrating
An anniversary.
People write letters
Expressing their views.
Sometimes the news is good,
And sometimes bad.
There's the sports page,
All the news of the
Local teams.
Sometimes there isn't
Much news.
But when it's not
Delivered
I do miss it.

H Costello

A New Day

Notes

For my son, Richard, who is autistic.

My name is Cheryl Mann, I am 41 and married to Steve. We have three children, Laura 23, Sarah 12 and Richard 5. I live in a quiet village called Llanhilleth in Gwent, South Wales.

I am a housewife and my hobbies are writing, reading, country walking and salt dough modelling.

I have been published in Poetry Now 94, Talking Volumes, Island Moods and Reflections, also several magazines.

I started writing about seven years ago when we moved to Wales from Essex. Usually it is feelings of great sadness or joy that inspire me and of course my family.

A new day, for a moment all is well,
Then I realise it's another day of worry, who can tell,
what will happen, happy games,
or frustration, it can be hell?
You have an angel's face
and a smile that lights my way,
but inside your little head
different pictures play.
I try to help but never know
if what I do is right.
Every day's a battle, every day's a fight.
If I could change places with you,
God only knows I would,
for you deserve a chance at life
you'd do great things if you could.
I can hold your hand my dear
and wipe your little tears.
I will be there always love
to help you through the years.
Until then we'll struggle on
together, hand in hand,
Along the road ahead
that fate for you has planned.

Cheryl Mann

Notes

This is my second poem to be published through Poetry Today. My first, *The Big Win*, can be found in Mists of Time.

It is difficult at the moment, to find free time, to write poems. Time spent in the private room of the house can prove very valuable. I like to use this time to reflect, or find answers to life's questions. So we should not waste this gift of time that nature gives us.

Paper Play

As I sit here on the throne
contemplating life
I think of my son and my
lovely wife

I think of my car, shining in the
sun
I think of my childhood and
endless fun

I ponder the future and what
lies ahead
Of past relationships and where
they might have led

I read the writing, left upon
the wall
Some letters big, some letters
small

Another job done, I must be
on my way
For ten minutes rest, there is
a price to pay

I have fallen foul to someone's
jolly caper
What should I do, they've hidden
the toilet paper.

Ian Dickerson

Best Boy

Man grown.
Out shopping with Mam.
Smiling 'hello'
to complete strangers.
Some smirk, some nod,
embarrassed, glance at Mam.
(Poor woman, they think)
'Man of the House,'
(Man says)
Washing up, makes the tea
for Mam.
Mam laughs,
She scolds,
She cries,
(Sometimes)
And you cuddle her,
Crying too,
Not knowing why.

It would be nice to think
that God smiles a special smile
for you.

S E Wright

Appleby - Heaven on Earth

Notes

I am 41 years old, married with two daughters aged 15 and 13. I am a self-employed builder and I live in Nottinghamshire. My hobbies are caravanning in the countryside, all sports and weight training.

I started writing at Christmas 1995 as I had been off work for a year with illness.

I like writing about the countryside and animals. I like writing about the seasons because there's so much happening in each season.

I'd like to dedicate this poem to Frank and Audrey Atkinson of Colby.

The sun-capped mountains look so serene
This clear day is a summer dream.
Hikers up winding paths tread
Arrive at peak their legs like lead.
Cows lie down in pastures green
So at peace or so it seems.
All you hear are natural sounds
Birds whistling their mates have found.
Hedges and trees are all in bloom
Flowers all over the fields strewn.
Telegraph poles and wires spread and stretch.
Across this field and into the next.
Some fields with silage some with crops
As far as one sees the fields never stop
Far off a chimney billowing smoke
Underneath a fire's being stoked.
No towns or motorways are here to spoil
Its as nature intended grass and soil
Mountains, hills and blue skies
Cows and sheep, birds in flight.
Rabbits scamper outside their burrows
Sun across the landscape roams.
The river flows beside bended trees
Under the bridge and through the reeds.
This place must be paradise
No place better none so nice.

Raymond Birch

Notes

I am Adele Hyndman, 30 years old and live in Edinburgh. I work as an HIV counsellor.

Poems so far published include: *Untitled* in Poets Corner, Anchor Books; *Daddy in* Words From Within, Anchor Books; *Letting Go* in A Passage in Time, *Paid in Kind*, Mists of Time. The International Society of Poets. Also several poems published in women's magazines. Editor's Choice Award for outstanding achievement in Poetry 1996 presented by The International Society of Poets.

Fairy Stories

When clouds were made of cotton wool
and fairies danced in rings
When cupid shot his bow and arrow
and you said such sweet things

When Sleeping Beauty awoke with a kiss
and the tooth fairy was fact
When Snow White found her own true prince
and love was still intact

When dreams came true and we believed
that love could really last
How could we know that fairy stories
were just a thing of the past.

Adele Hyndman

Feelings

I didn't know when
I was a girl I knew
I didn't want to hurt
you, and as I grew I
knew right from wrong
but I wanted someone
a friend a boy, a man
and yes to be a good
wife, have babies to, all
that has gone now - it took
me so long to see that
from now on and till I
die I must follow
my heart my life must
be for me I know
this is right and each
time I breath in the
fresh air now that I'm
free I now know
the path you must take
must be your own that's
why I was born, yes
to be me.

Gaynor Louise

Solitary Walk

Notes

I am a 47 year old housewife with a grown up family of four.

My hobbies, besides writing poetry, are reading, gardening, driving and tapestry.

This is the second poem I have entered. I have written poetry from my schooldays but never kept any of them until recently.

To the question of what inspires me to write, all I can say is that something will come into my head and I will write it down and the words will just come together. It is something that just comes naturally.

Take a solitary walk along the beach
Let the wind blow the cobwebs from your mind
Listen to the thunder of crashing waves
And leave all your troubles behind

Hear the gulls scream as they fly overhead
Fighting the wind as they soar
Watch the clouds being blown away
Like your problems, they're not there anymore

Sit on the sand dunes and rest awhile
Think of happy things not sad
Close your eyes and let your mind drift
Then you'll see, life isn't all bad

You'll feel strong once more and peaceful inside
And know that things are within reach
Able to face whatever's in store
Thanks to the walk on the beach

Susan Prescott

I Remember

I remember your lovely young face fresh as the morning dew
I remember slipping a ring on your finger when our love was new
I remember a newly wed, setting out on married life
I remember the vows exchanged that made us man and wife
I remember a young bride hand in mine all dressed in white
Full of true love by day and full of passion at night
I remember our first born, a boy followed by a cute little girl
I remember thinking life's perfect in our little family world
I remember driving to hospital to honour the consultant's tryst
I remember the shock and the horror when he reported a cyst
I remember your vitality, your love of life how you learned to be a good
                                                            dancer
I remember how you loved me and the children before they said it was
                                                            cancer
I remember the cortege and the pain, the tears and the prayers we did in
                                                            tone
I remember crying in the rain and seeing your name hewn on a headstone
I remember the children were brave, too shocked I think to cry
I remember they kept asking me why their mummy had to die
I remember saying, when a life so good as your mother's God decides to
                                                            take
I can only think he's so overworked God sometimes makes a mistake

Alan Sharrock

The Rat Race

Notes

I'm 65, married to Derek for 40 years, sadly, no children. I've lived in the same Yorkshire village all my life and worked in accounts, as a VDU operator and as first-aid nurse until made redundant in my early fifties.

I have a wide range of interests, enjoy motor-cycling, both on my little scooter, and riding pillion on our big Yamaha, reading, swimming, photography, gardening and organising our local 'Meals on Wheels' service.

I love to travel, have been as far afield as New Zealand and the USA, an interest helped by being a devoted fan of opera singer José Carreras, whom I travel to see and hear when and wherever possible.

I've been writing poems for family and friends' special occasions for many years but only recently have tried my hand at more general poetry.

The pleasure I've had listening to José and his music has been the inspiration behind several of my poems, plus being fortunate to live in a lovely area of the country. Otherwise almost anything can start me thinking of a theme for a new one. I've had several published in the last couple of years, so I must be getting something right!

Hustle, bustle, race and dash,
Schedules to keep, and trains to catch.
No time to watch the world go by,
No minute to spare, just have to fly!
But to what end is all this haste,
Going through life at this hectic pace?
No time to see beauty all around,
Or hear birdsong, drowned 'neath traffic sound?
So busy rushing from day to day,
We miss all the beautiful sights on the way.
And what do you gain, along with the cash?
But ulcers through stress, and then heart attacks!
So slow down, take it easy, life isn't a race,
Look around, for the world is a wonderful place,
That oak tree was there, before you were born,
And will still be there, long after you've gone!
Now relax and enjoy life, for I've heard it said,
And it's true, that you'll be a long time dead!

Kathleen Adams

Notes

I am a twice-widowed lady, now enjoying the status of a senior citizen, who derives much enjoyment from both reading and writing poetry. I find it provides escapism from today's violent world.

I have been writing poetry since 1988 (following the death of my second husband).

In 1993 I became a member of a local Writers' Group. Both before and since joining the group I have had my poems accepted for nine different anthologies and a few have been published in magazines.

Nature's Balm was written after I had spent an enjoyable weekend with dear friends whose bungalow is sited alongside the river. I am always able to *recharge my batteries* when I visit.

Many things inspire me to write poetry - the wondrous effect of a sunset - moonlight on the water, or perhaps just an ordinary everyday event sparks off a turn of phrase and it 'snowballs' from there.

Nature's Balm

The sweet enchantment of a summer evening
Along the riverbank
In solitude I stroll
Savouring the tranquillity -
'At one' with nature -
A rabbit scuttles past into his hole.

Trout are 'rising'
Rippling the water,
A heron, statuesque
Surveys the scene -
The tensions of my day
Fast disappearing
And 'senior' reverts to 'seventeen.'

Doreen Conway-Haynes

This poem was inspired by an ex-girlfriend's passion for bingo. I went with her a few times and listened to the caller with interest. Unfortunately our relationship wasn't to last and my brief involvement with bingo died with our love. Still at least one good thing came out of it, I won a prize for this poem, which is more than I ever won at bingo!

Of course there's a very good chance Mr Major may not have his *Den* anymore at number ten when you read this but at the time of writing it seems like he will be there for eternity!

Bingo

I heard the call
It's Major's Den
And crossed away
My number ten
The caller then said
Here's Legs Eleven
I didn't need that
I wanted seven
I needed two more
To complete a line
Where's Anyway Up
Where's Sixty Nine
Unlucky for some
Number Thirteen
I'm getting further
From my dream
Key of the door
Twenty One
I cross it off
No, that's wrong
On its own
Number Seven
Only one to get
I'm near heaven
The jackpot's mine
I know I'll win
I don't care
If greed's a sin
House
Please wait for the check
The caller utters
All I can do
Is curse and mutter
The winner was lucky
His cards were hot
His numbers came up
He won the pot
But maybe next game
The prize will be mine
If I get the four corners
Or any straight line

Paul Duddles

Notes

My other published works include: *All Alone am I,* published by Poetry Now's, *Love lines,* spring 1995, *Please Take Me Home,* published May 1996 by International Society of Poets. *In Memory of Steven,* published in *Mists of Time* by Poetry Today, autumn 1996. I also received The Editors Choice Award by the International Society of Poets 1996.

I have four children, Micheal, Maria, Amanda and Gemma. My mum's name is Mrs Renee Lawton and I dedicate the poem to my dad, Mr Sidney Daniel Lawton, known as Danny, who passed away on 23rd August 1995, whom I love and miss very much but I know he is with me in spirit helping me to write better and better poems. Could I also mention my sister Denise and her husband Mick and their children Lisa and Sam. I love all my family and just want them all to know that.

Dad, You Won't Be There

You were the best dad, that ever there was,
I'll always love you just because
You were always there, when I needed you
We didn't always speak, but you always knew.

I'll always love and remember you
The childhood memories, will always be there,
You were a part of me growing up
The one man I knew that would care.

And now you're finally resting, in heaven up above,
You'll finally meet Steven, please give him all my love,
We all will love and miss you
One day together we will be
Never to be parted for all eternity.

So I'll remember you singing
And I'll remember you cared
I'll turn around hoping
But I know you won't be there.

Susan Elizabeth Senior

One Day of My Life . . .

Notes

Since being published in 1996 for the first time, I have basked in the praise (and witnessed the astonishment!) of my family, friends and colleagues. But, seeing my own lines in print urged me to read other people's achievements and, by so doing, found myself being cut back down to size. One aspect *did* gratify me in that many seem to use poetry as a method of expressing their emotions when no other outlet appears available. Like myself!

Pushing sixty, the time is approaching when I should be able to indulge my 'hobby' in a far more relaxed fashion and do more profound and meaningful pieces which would be inspiring and uplifting to any who might do me the honour of reading them - my original dream!

I feel at present that I let the pace and pressures of life overtake me - this is reflected in *One Day of my Life . . .* but that is now, who knows what's to come.

I have three lovely little grandchildren, Thomas, Joe and Kathryn, and possibly with the opportunity of relaxing with them more often it will enable me to produce a happier style of writing, less introspective than hitherto.

The radio gently awakens me from my sleep
My eyes flicker, my mind begins to ponder
On the day ahead, what has it in its keep?
What is in store for me? I pause to wonder.

I doze while I plan my day, while I plot,
My brain already writing a mental list
Of my responsibilities, the desires I've got
Taking second place to the duties that persist

I come to the end of the time I enjoy
Whilst putting off that moment at which I must give
All my time and energy to those who employ
Me to work for them, *slave* for them, in order to live.

There's no use dallying for the moment has come
For me to rise from my bed and tackle the day.
I get myself ready - now is everything done?
Is the house left all tidy? Yes! I'm on my way!

From home to office - the roadworks! The traffic!
Changing roles from wife to Secretary PA
The computer on my desk just waiting for a flick
Of a switch, to bring the screen into play.

There are 'phone calls and letters and accounts to be typed.
There are also the clients, whom I like to greet
With a cup of coffee, before smiles are wiped
From their faces on seeing their Balance Sheet!

The work is not hard - sometimes even a bore,
When having to detail all the work which is done.
Each hour of the day to be accounted for
From eight thirty 'til five, when it's time to go home.

The minute I leave the office behind
And start walking to join up with my darling man,
All accountancy work is dismissed from my mind
As we meet and get home as fast as we can!

There's a meal to prepare - evening baths to be had
Then a drink to help us both settle down
To a evening relaxing, which makes us feel glad
It's the end of the day, when time is our own!

For five days of the week we are ruled by the clock
And stuck in our grooves doing the same old things
But weekends are the times when at work we can mock
And enjoy life as we should with the joys freedom brings

Ros Silom

Poesy Indeed

Notes

I am a retired Head of Shrewsbury School of Art, aged 79 years, married and have a son and daughter. Our daughter is married and has two children.

My hobbies include collecting historic porcelain, and antiques generally. I am keen on the analysis of the history of architecture and modern architectural design.

I started to write poetry about four years ago, for personal interest. I have always had some imaginative ideas regarding painting and design and now I appreciate that writing, especially poetry, does not involve the secondary struggle and anguish of manipulating an intervening medium, one thinks of something and just writes it down!

I have had one poem published by The International Society of Poets which was shortlisted for a prize. I have written a history of the Shrewsbury School of Art to commemorate its 125th anniversary, a copy of which is retained in the local authority reference library, and a few short articles for charity, published by the North Wales and Shropshire Hospice.

A life hard packed with reason
Gaining an inch a day some days;
The lottery of living within cause and effect
Can't it be by-passed some ways?

A life within a life the one and the other,
Life's reality versed into biblical terms
Like God's six days of arranging -
By magic - and the scientist squirms!

That creative remiss - if only I had thought of that!
It's never too late to hitch a thoughtful lift
And grab some loose phrase, copyright free,
Bringing the universe into a neat shift

As the air is full of quick, quiet words
Internetting electro-magnetic waves,
Winging all about us, through us -
Statutory rights completely waived!

The scientist researches resolution to mysteries
Back, back, forward in time - everything's turning out rosy,
Except that vital, ultimate equation
Which, despite analysis, dissipates into poesy!

J R Lucas

Notes

My full name is Trevor Howard Vincent, I was born 11
November 1955 in Temple-
combe, Somerset.

I live in Lovington, a very
small village in Somerset, I
have lived in Somerset all of
my life.

I am an ardent follower of
Yeovil Town FC, my hobbies
are watching sport on the
television and writing poetry.

I began writing poems about
12 years ago, only recently
have I had any published. I
have hand written more than
2,000 poems and store them
in hardback writing books.

Poetry to me is about everyday life, about imagination.
Out of Hand is about children
with access to matches and
the dangers.

I hope to one day see all my
poems in print and published
in books.

Out of Hand

One day the sofa, a farm became
kids with toy tractors, a farming game
they call this place cardboard farm
ah, thought mum, can come to no harm
there was silage made, in cushion field
cows in the shed after giving milk yield
now, mum was a smoker, the door was shut
there was stubble, where the grass was cut
the tallest child was now stretching himself
he pulled mother's matches, down from the shelf
when he struck the match, the flame was bright
he set light to the stubble which did ignite
but the flame quickly spread to the rest of the farm
the threat was real so there was much harm
mum was outside, having a smoke
the heat cracked a window the kids did choke
she walked through the kitchen, in through the door
then horror befell her, charred bones on the floor
so the three healthy kids who farmed in toyland
perished in their game that got out of hand . . .

Trevor Vincent

Notes

Mollie Holmes Stocks lives with her retired husband Bryan in a quiet and leafy suburb of Bristol. They have three grown up children and two grandchildren.

Her interest in poetry grew during the war as she read The Rubaiyat of Omar Khayyam, translated by Edward Fitzgerald.

'Lights Out' in a wooden ATS hut meant Mollie reciting, to herself, many of her favourite Khayyam's philosophical poems. It was much more enjoyable than the supposedly soporific counting of sheep.

Given the pleasant task of writing other peoples' nostalgic memories, in poem form, is the rewarding and fun element for Mollie.

She has always enjoyed sketching which has been a lifetime hobby.

A Bit of Psychology

The sage once said
The grass grew greener,
When one had to face
The leaving of this arena.

And didn't another state
The obvious,
We become wiser the older
And it ought to be the opposite.

If we were wiser when the younger -
Strife and war and such the like
We'd deal with better - not be the
Bungler.

M H Stocks

Notes

Being recently widowed, I live in Abergele, North Wales.

I have now had five poems put in anthologies and three in a newspaper. It has been my life line and made many friends for me.

Please dedicate this to my lovely husband Albert, who was so supportive.

Tolerance

Some people are dark
Some are fair
Some have straight or curly hair.

Eyes of green's, brown's or blue's
Skins of all the different hues.
Different cultures here and there
'So what' that's everyone's own affair.

Some people are *always* on the go
Others really very slow,
They want to go at their own pace
They don't want to join that Old Rat Race.

So sister to sister, brother to brother,
Let us learn to live with each other,
Cos if you put us all in one big pot
Give it a stir 'what have you got?'

There'd be *one* colour, creed and race
We'd all come out with just one face!

Margaret Toft

Notes

Tony Tipper is 50 years of age. He has worked in The National Museum of Wales in Cardiff for 33 years; where he is responsible for the curation of vascular plants and timbers. He also looks after a collection of over 20,000 postage stamps on botanical themes and puts on bi-monthly exhibitions for the public.

His Finnish wife, Sini-Marjut, was a pen-friend before they got married in Helsinki in 1969. They have one daughter called Annabelle.

His love of poetry dates back over thirty years and he has written 500 poems to date. He puts his inspiration down to his love of nature and for the romantic poets including John Clare, John Keats and Samuel Taylor Coleridge.

His hobbies include stamp collecting and an interest in memorabilia of Newport County Football Club. He has also successfully completed numerous long-distance walks including the 600 mile South West Way and has climbed all of Wainwright's 214 Lake District fells. He is also a keen supporter of Merthyr Tydfil Football Club.

Miracle of Sense

Wind blow, wind flow,
Through the summer corn.
Corn sow, corn grow,
Before the mighty storm.

Rain fall, rain soak,
The barren land of drought.
Drought go, water flow,
Man cannot live without.

Food give, food save,
The children of this earth.
Earth thank, earth bless,
This miracle of sense.

Tony Tipper

Moving

Notes

I am aged 65, widowed with four children and two grandchildren. I was born in London, evacuated during the war to Weston-super-Mare and now live in Banwell, nearby. I am an ex-GPO telephonist.

My home and family are very special to me, I enjoy reading, writing, poetry, arranging flowers, walking, playing bingo and music.

I have written poetry for some years, from school days really, although I have not yet had other works published. I am inspired to write by such things as the tenacity of ordinary people, the elements, the beauty of the universe, or loneliness.

The inspiration came for this poem when moving house last summer.

I should like to dedicate this poem to my family.

Boxes packed to overflowing
Dogs barking
Cats Meowing
'Alright we haven't forgotten you
You are coming with us too'
Cancel milk - cut off the gas
Don't forget that old chest
Endless books and clothes and shoes
Pictures, bric-a-brac old news
Read the meters
Pay the bills
'What's that on the window sill?'
A photograph - 'Oh yes, take that'
It is my favourite snap.
'Be careful how you carry that'
Will we make it on time
Old house - sad to leave you behind
I've tendered you through all these years
You've seen all my joy and tears
Now the time has come to go
Bless those who loved you so
Bring the new ones love and health
And happiness and wealth.

Catherine Frost

Notes

I am forty eight years old, mother of three children now aged twenty four, twenty one and ten. I married Derek Holmes in July 1993 (3rd time lucky!). He's now the love of my life. I moved around with the British Forces (Army) for thirty two years, and have now lived in Dukinfield near Manchester since 1987.

I had credits at college (1980s) for creative writing and have had three poems published. My hobbies are: singing, songwriting, poetry and children's stories, and writing to pen-pals. I have been writing since I was at Secondary School. I am inspired by life, nature, emotions- everything.

I've dedicated this poem to mum and dad Parker, who live in Onchan, Isle of Man. They truly are the best parents, and I really do love them both so very much.

Mum and Dad

Dear Mum and Dad - I'm hoping - my poem, will convey,
Just - how much, I love you, in every single way;
You both mean the world to me, without you - I'd be sad,
Because, you're . . . 'Oh! So special,' my loving - Mum and Dad.

You comfort me, with cuddles and shower me, with kisses,
I hope, I am a credit, to your future hopes and wishes;
You listen to my problems and give me . . . inspiration,
So, I'm writing this, to tell the world, you're the 'best in the nation.'

A J Holmes

From Darkness

Notes

I am Jennifer Walsh, aged 51, separated with two grown up children. I work as a telephonist in West Sussex.

I started writing poetry as therapy during a very traumatic period of my life.

My hobbies are gardening, reading, travel, theatre, writing and art.

I have written occasionally since school, mainly stories and poems relating to memorable events and days over the years. I have been writing seriously for about two years.

My inspiration comes from how I originally felt each day. Now my life has improved I can appreciate what's around me. I write about daily happenings, nature and the world around us.

For all, there are times when the world is a dark and lonely place,
When all you have fought for, now seems a waste.
Some days when life seems full of hope.
Some days when you will feel unable to cope.
So be strong on the days you are alone and sad.
Enjoy those days that are neither good or bad.
Be thankful, for all around, there are many pleasures to see.
Then from the darkness, you will walk free.

Days once so bright, now are no longer here.
Sad times must be allowed to gently disappear.
Those dreams once cherished now are lost
For lost dreams, we pay some kind of cost.
Then, come times, when you are courageous and strong
When a happy smile, a kind word are not wrong.
Though deep within pain and tears are still there
To the world, you pretend not to care.
A future both bright and new, waits for all
Who can find strength and refuse to fall.
Don't let pain and sadness take from you and me
That day, when from darkness we can walk free.

Such gifts freely given are yours to keep
May past pain and future joy never meet.
If they do, then lessons learnt are such a waste.
Each day, brings new challenges to be faced.
Once conquered, the fear's all gone
One more step on the road that seems so long.
There is a new life to greet, new sights to see.
When from such darkness you will walk free.

Jennifer Walsh

Time

Tick - tock, tick - tock,
Goes the lonely old clock,
He waits for no one, he's a job to do,
Day and night, morning and noon,
Does a day ever stop and time stand still,
For him it starts where it ends, a day to fill.

It's oh so quiet except for the sound,
Of the second hand ticking round and round,
For me the night grows longer as I watch,
The big hand become slower as it moves notch to notch,
How funny time flies when you're having fun,
And oh how it drags when you're having none.

I look from my window out into the night,
But see nothing and no one, try as I might,
I'll look again when time can then see,
The beginning of a new day, waiting for me,
But now I must sleep, yes at last,
As present is near and yesterday has past.

Julieanne Boyle

I was born in Newcastle-upon-Tyne on 15 January 1937.

I was adopted when I was nine months old. My adopted mother died when I was 19 months old. My adopted father had to join the Durham Light Infantry to fight in the war; I never saw him again until I was seven years old.

I was brought up in his absence by family friends who had no children of their own; I loved them dearly.

I moved to Yorkshire when I was eight years old when my adopted father remarried.

I was married at 20 years old and had three sons and two daughters. I then felt complete, a proper family of my own to love. We are a wonderful, close family. I have eight grandchildren who are my pride and joy.

I work as a telephone sales consultant for a Yorkshire brewery. I have been writing poetry for a number of years for friends and family. This is the first year I have entered any for publication. I have a poem, entitled 'The Smile', that has been chosen for the finals in the autumn.

People inspire me to write, their happiness, their sadness, affects me, I need to put my feelings into words.

My interests are my family's achievements, pride in my grandchildren, the happiness we share together.

I would like to continue with my writing, my dream is to write a series for TV. The ideas are there in my head, who knows what's in store for me?

My Love's My Life

My love's my life,
My heart fills with pride,
As I watch you grow,
Your achievements and dreams,
I love you so,
Each one so different,
Yet alike,
Angels one minute,
The next you're tykes,
So innocent, so happy,
Trusting and bright,
I want to protect you,
Day and night,
Beautiful little faces,
Uplifted for a kiss,
Being a grandma is utter bliss.

Lilian Roundhill

The Lattice Window

Waiting in the queue before lights of red
Drumming fingers upon steering wheel
Something made me look up and I saw you
Waving grey haired from a lattice window

Why were you waving I wondered worried?
I thought you couldn't be waving to me
Unless you'd mistaken the car I drive
For that of a friend or your family

Then I noticed the sign above the door
No family abode before me there
But a residential nursing home
It dawned on me then you must be in care

Who was it you were waving to and why
Was it some husband, lover, brother, son
A farewell as he leaves to serve his land
Never to return though the war is won?

Red lights changed first flashing amber then green
The journey ahead only just begun
I hoped you could see me as I waved for
You could be my mother and I your son

Steve Chester

The Cool Cats

Notes

Andrea Maddox is 41 years of age, and has two daughters aged 13 and 9.

She has had a short story called *A Simple Diagnosis* published, together with a poem entitled *Housewife's Lament*.

She writes about everyday people and their feelings and experiences: the woman in the supermarket, the tramp in the shop doorway, the shabby wayward child. She has been writing since she was 12, with mixed success but Andrea says it will never put her off if she is not always successful with her work.

Writing is the best therapy she knows for just about everything. As soon as she gets an idea, she rushes to the typewriter, whether for a poem or a story, to make sure she doesn't lose the 'feeling' for it. She is currently writing a novel called *The Dandelion Clock*.

Feline all of them.
Armed with talons, used like claws,
They'll scratch your eyes out,
Then lick their paws.

In the dark they ply their wares,
Trapping the lads into their lairs.
I move hopefully into their patch.
Their eyes harden, they're ready to scratch.

I move away. I know the score.
It works like a charm and they want more.
It's no good using a winsome look.
They collect the scalps. They wrote the book.

Dresses split from ankle to thigh.
There's no contest, I'm too shy.
Give in girl. It's not worth a jot.
The Cool Cats are ready to give all they've got.

But just a minute, one's broken away.
He's made his escape and he's heading my way.
A smile of relief crosses his face.
'You're so ugly darlin' I know I'm safe!'

Andrea Maddox

To My Husband

Notes

Known by most people as 'Rene,' I am an average sort of person, very easy going and friendly. Now 61, I have been married to Ray for 42 years, and lived in Saltash most of my life. We have six children, and, at the last count, 15 grandchildren, number 15 is now 4 month old, and number 1 great-grandchild due in March.

Formerly a Nursery Nurse, I worked for many years with handicapped children. I now do occasional relief work, as a Warden with retired Naval people.

I love reading, and entering competitions, and of course, sometimes writing poetry! I was always fairly good at rhyming, but my earliest prize was at the age of 16, when the Town Council held a contest to celebrate Elizabeth becoming Queen. Usually, my poems are about my feelings, or events and people close to me. In the last year, I have been lucky enough to have two poems selected for the semi-finals, in contests held by the International Society of Poets; both will have been published (in separate books) by the autumn of this year. Sadly, having heard no more, I presume I didn't make it to the finals! I have also had poems published in other books in this series.

A loving husband and wonderful dad,
the very best grandad anyone had,
You worked hard all of your life
Caring for children, home and wife.
Now, over sixty, and work is slack,
things are going wrong behind your back,
No work, no money, just puzzle and worry,
Pray for a pools' win - wish it would hurry!
Car's going wrong and it's making a noise,
Can't even go for a drink with the boys!
Really depressed, impatient and blue -
Wish there was something that *I* could do.
What if I won a wonderful prize?
Would *that* bring the sparkle back to your eyes?
That trip of a lifetime, to Egypt, for two,
(The cruise on the Nile, just me and you!)
And any cash over the bills we would pay,
So you could stop worrying right away,
And once more, be a loving husband and dad,
And the very best grandad anyone had.

Irene M Standlick

The Spider

There's a spider on my ceiling,
And he's looking down at me.
I don't know why he's watching,
What does he hope to see?

He's been up there all through Brookside,
And through the Live Big Fight,
He's brown and very hairy,
I hope he doesn't bite.

Perhaps I ought to kill him,
To squash him with my shoe,
Or if I could just catch him,
I could flush him down the loo.

Just a minute, now he's moving,
He's running down the wall,
I could guide him through the doorway,
And out into the hall.

He's out there now, that's better,
He's a big one, that's for sure,
It's not that I'm still frightened,
But I think I'll lock the door.

Steven Millhouse

The Flower Seller

Notes

I am 49 years old, married with two grown-up sons and live in East London where I was born. My occupation is a post office counter clerk.

My hobbies include writing, reading, country walks, going to the theatre, and cooking.

My interest in poetry began at school, inspired by famous poets like Longfellow and Keats, followed in recent years by Pam Ayres and Patience Strong.

On the corner of the street stands Bella
She's old and plump and a flower seller,
In a long black dress and lacy shawl
With a smile on her face, and mornin' to all.
'Roses for a loved one,' is her cry,
'Come and see, come and buy.'
Sweet smelling fragrance all in a row,
Bunches of flowers tied with a bow.
Blooms of beautiful colours - oh so bright!
Lilies, carnations, freesia too,
'A posy dear - just for you.'
You will find her standing there everyday,
Bella - the famous flower seller.

Susan Baxter

Notes

I was born in Birmingham, 3 November 1940, my parents are Edward and Violet Crook. I am married to Derek George Matthews, we have three children, Jacqueline, Annette and Philip, and six grandchildren, Katie, Lauren, Jay, Liam, Joseph and Jessica. I have lived in Swansea in Glamorgan since I was three years old.

I am a retired sales consultant, and am a member of the local Women's Institute and patron of the local Operatic Society.

I started writing poetry last year, in May 1996, and have written twenty two poems in nine months. Ten of my poems have been accepted for publication in anthologies called; The Other Side of the Mirror, Between a Laugh and a Tear, Quiet Moments, Awaken to a Dream, Jewels of the Imagination and A Lasting Calm for the International Library of Poetry. Also two of my poems, *Determination* and *So Wonderful* have been taped for The Sound of Poetry. Two more of my poems have just recently been accepted for publication by Forward Press and Vale Publishing. I've been published in Mists of Time and now Day by Day.

I usually write about the trials of life, and there is sometimes a hidden message within them, which I hope the reader can understand.

Sport Mad

What is wrong with me? I ask - my heart cries out,
Why! am I left alone again . . . I shout,
I do my best to be his friend and wife,
He tells me that I am the centre of his life.

But, what is wrong with me? I cry - trying *not* to be a bore,
As he goes off to play the game of *golf*, he loves much more,
He is the only one I want, and I love *his* company,
I tell him this, he smiles, agrees, but still drives off the *tee*.

I feel so lonely when he's gone, my hands across my breasts,
You see I only want to be with him, and I have no other interests,
I sit and wait and read a book, until at last he comes home,
I'm only happy when I'm with him, and I do *not* wish to roam.

He never even thought of *golf*, when he was courting me,
It was football, rugby and cricket then, as well as my company,
I wish I had realised years ago, that it would be like this,
I'd have married a man that hated *sport*, and only loved to *kiss*.

I thought he would have hung up his clubs by now, 'I don't know why?'
He told me, that *on the golf course*, is where he wished to die,
How stupid I am, to sit and wait, these thoughts inside my head,
Imagining that he *really wants* to be with *me* instead.

Joan Yvonne Matthews

Notes

I'm 17 now and have been writing poems for many years. To me it seems to be the easiest and most effective way of expressing my feelings.

I live in a small quiet town where nothing much happens and so trivial things seem to mean so much more here. My inspiration comes from these events and feelings and from everybody else around me.

So Hard isn't dedicated to any one person, but more all those who can read and identify with it.

I have now had quite a number of my poems published into various anthologies and this, along with pressure, help and encouragement from friends and family, has encouraged me to continue writing and to send off other works.

So Hard

They screen it in the movies,
They act it in the plays,
It seems like love is everything these days.

They broadcast it on TV,
It's on the radio,
Everybody has love but we're prone to let it go.

'Cos it's too hard to hold,
And it's too hard to keep,
It'll brighten up your darkest days but never let you sleep.

You hear it on the telephone,
It's on your channel four,
It should only be on after nine, a crime if shown before.

Then you wouldn't have to hurt yourself,
By flicking to your favourite show,
To hear all the couples so happy about the one thing in life
You let go.

'Cos it's so hard to hold,
And it's so hard to keep,
That if it brightens up a cloudy day,
You can wave goodbye to sleep.

Aleena Matthews

Notes

I live in Cornwall with my husband Richard and son David, having moved seven years ago from quite close to Boscobel, famous for the oak tree in which Charles II hid.

I have written poetry for only two years, my favourite poet being William Blake.

I try to write simply but with deep meaning with often religious connotations, but enjoy nature and the seasons.

My own book of poetry is to be published soon and children's story books in the autumn.

Happy Homes

Like people, houses have their own distinction,
An old Georgian type, many floors with definitely no extension.
It looks austere but noble, stands above the rest,
Many windows all of sashes, small panes that show off the best.

The little terraced house, in a 19th century row,
Some tiny rooms, two up, two down, no bath or loo to go.
They look so friendly joined together with neighbours very close,
Over the wall housewives gossip, rather loud of voice.

A modern detached house with gardens front and rear
Stands alone, upright and strong, built with shops quite near.
The semi is a funny type, just half a detached plot,
It has same rooms as detached, but shares a chimney pot.

My favourite is the thatch like a cosy woolly hat,
White-washed walls, lattice windows, with welcome front door mat.
A wild and pretty garden a friendly natural plan,
With bees and butterflies, a peaceful house for man.

The bungalow is half the height, a funny squat affair,
All the rooms on one floor, no need for rise of stair.
A pretty level garden for those who cannot climb,
The bungalow is perfect for your retirement time.

Lucy-may Bloxham

Mother Mine

My mother believed
Power of love
Power of pray
Brotherhood of man

Tender hand to furrowed brow
Power from the touch
Constant giver of all

Heed the still voice listen to this
That body and mind withstand
One of a few waked this way
This gracious lady.

Mary Hughes

Notes

I am married to Andrew, we have two daughters, Sharon and Roslyn, both married. We have two grandchildren, Rachel and Alexander.

I was educated at Fraserburgh North Primary School and then Fraserburgh Academy. I work in retail ladies' fashions and am a school supervisor.

My poetry has been published by the National Library of Poetry in America, which is affiliated to the National Library of Poetry, London and Kent. Also by Arrival Press, Peterborough, and Triumph House, Peterborough

Inspiration

To be inspired by what you see
Making thoughts a reality
The garden in bloom beautiful to see
The gardener's busy planting plants is he
Can I do that - can I do that
A teacher learning pupils new
Eager to learn they like school too
Can I do that - can I do that
A singer singing on a stage of blue
Quite a performance and for you
Can I do that - can I do that
A builder building a house so fine
For a family to live in they think it's divine
Can I do that - can I do that
Transporting people to destinations a far
On a boat a train or fast moving plane
Can I do that - can I do that
Authors they do write their books
Hoping their readers will do more than look
Can I do that - can I do that
Writing poetry far into the night
What pleasure poets give they give delight
I can do that - I can do that
Inspiration it fills my head
There is quite a lot that can be said
But my thoughts I've written down instead

Sheila MacDonald

Notes

Sue Carter-Gadd is a 36 years old mother of two boys, Oliver and Sebastian, who embarked on a writing course in July of this year. Since then she has had three poems published in various anthologies. Sue lives in Clevedon, Somerset, which is a 'poetic' place: Thackeray wrote some of his poetry there; Coleridge lived in Clevedon for some time; Hallam lived there also and his death inspired Tennyson to write *In Memoriam*.

The inspiration for her first poem came from the birth of her first son, Oliver. Further inspiration comes from everyday situations.

Her ambition is to write a novel based on life's experiences and she is hoping to continue having her work published through her writing course.

Reflections

I look in the mirror and what do I see,
A familiar face staring at me.
It has been with me for thirty six years,
Through fun and laughter, pain and tears,
It has been my friend and sometimes my foe,
It is with me wherever I go.
Wherever I go - whatever the place,
It's kind of consoling this familiar face.
My life has been busy, involved and complicated,
But me and my persona have always related.
If I am sad I look and I smile,
And I will be happy if only for a while.
The feelings my countenance can portray,
Will be with me night and day.
As I grow older out come more creams,
To keep my visage young, as in my dreams.
Let's hope this face of today is the face of tomorrow,
With lots of happiness and not much sorrow.

Sue Carter-Gadd

Notes

I am a 72 years old retired married lady living in Kidlington, Oxon, on the edge of the Cotswolds. I have a daughter and son and a grand-daughter.

I have had about 50 poems published in various anthologies, including 'A Passage in Time' and 'Voices on the Wind' by the International Society of Poets. So far my prizes add up to the princely sum of £48.00, made up of small awards for poems published in Poetry Magazines and a National Magazine. Currently my main hobby is writing poetry, But I also enjoy solving crosswords and reading.

My first poem was inspired about ten years ago by a painting done by my sister, Pam Harper, a talented artist

I wrote *Henley Regatta* after talking to a friend who had, himself, rowed at Henley in the recent past.

I have been inspired by many things, people, places, events, pets, sights, sounds, other peoples verses, the list is endless. I have now had a book of my own poems, *Pieces of My Mind,* published and hope to publish another one at the end of the year.

Henley Regatta

Eights and fours and coxless pairs
Show their prowess here,
Henley is their Mecca
It calls them every year.

All of them are at full stretch
As records they contest,
They skim along the river
Each striving to be best.

Each man puts his heart and soul
Into every race,
Content that he has done his best
To gain the coveted place.

Edna Cosby

My Brother and I

Notes

I am aged 34 and live in the North West of England and have two children aged 4 and 2 years respectively.

I started writing poetry in June 1996 initially for the children. Since then it has developed into thermodynamic and conservational poetry.

My interests are renewable energy and organic farming and conservation.

Hobbies include music, reading and lazy hazy sunny days with the family.

The inspiration for *My Brother and I* came from the children.

I am presently having a number of poems illustrated with a view to publishing.

I would like to dedicate this poem to all children everywhere.

I am a little girl
And I am only four
I like to run, and play about
And sometimes slam the door

I have a little brother
He is only two
And if he sees you coming
He will shout and wave to you

We have a mum and dad
And they're so nice to us
If we're very good some days
They take us on the bus

It is a great big red bus
It has an upstairs too
And if we see you stood outside
We'll shout and wave to you

We have a little pussycat
He's old, and black, and soft
We played a trick on him one day
And locked him in the loft

Mum and Dad were very cross
When they found what we had done
We're not to do that again
For the cat it's not much fun

M P Boylan

Notes

I am 17 years old and in the first year of my A level course. I am studying History, English Language and German at Great Barr GM Sixth Form. I also attended Great Barr school and achieved nine GCSE's, eight grade A and one grade B.

I write poetry for pleasure. I usually write from my own experience or take things that I see on television.

Roses

Sunshine, lazy mornings, a first kiss
Loud music, ice-cream, a birthday wish
A good book, a tear of joy, a guy's eyes
A wedding day under cloudless skies
Holding hands, phone calls, the smell of the sea
A faithful friend and being free
Red roses, summer nights, a child's birth
Every beautiful thing on earth.

Stephanie Locke

The Quiet Life

Memories,
Sweet memories,
Of youthful days
And happy ways.
Of loud guitars
And battered cars,
Of skating rinks,
Non alcohol drinks.
Bikini sands
In other lands.
The clinking glass,
The hours that pass
Till home again.
Bed at ten,
To start at work.
We mustn't shirk.
The years gone by,
And here am I
Retired at last.
Time flies fast,
But still there's so
Much to do, and Oh,
I don't know how
I managed now
To work all day
And still to play.
For my time's full
And never dull.
I ride my horses,
Go on courses,
Bake my cakes.
The time it takes!
Do the garden.
I beg your pardon,
I know it's not neat,
But, not to be beat
I plant the flowers
And weed for hours.
No trouble and strife,
It's not a bad life.

Dorothea B Kent

Notes

My name is James C Finnie, I am 47, divorced and a single parent with three children. A CNC machinist from Irvine in Ayrshire.

I play golf and have many varied interests.

I started writing poems at about the age of 14, and have written hundreds. Usually it is about an event that has happened, it may be very trivial, but if there is a laugh to be derived from it I will put pen to paper, and depending on the length of the poem it may take five minutes to one hour to compile.

Untitled

I thought I'd live my life and take the easy route
Everything in the garden's rosy, that's what life's about
But as everyone knows, fate sometimes takes its turn
You have no spare cash, no nothing to burn
But tomorrow is another day, it can only get better
It's coming up to bill time, oh that dreaded letter
Sure enough, as dependable as the morning rain
It's bigger than I thought, last month all over again
Someday, somehow, something will have to give
Is this life I'm living worth it to really live
But thanks for the faith of that man high above
An answer to my prayer, I've found a twenty in a glove
So it will be paid, I can breath again
I must get thrifty like all the rich men
Save a penny today, tomorrow it may be a pound
But where's this wise guy, when the bill's come around

James Finnie

Notes

I am 28 years old and was recently married to Bill. We live in a quiet village in the mountains of North Wales with our Border Collie dog, Bryn.

I am currently unemployed due to long term health problems, but have done voluntary work for the National Trust for a number of months and I'm hoping to go to college this year, firstly to embark upon a Welsh language course, as my knowledge of the language is somewhat limited at present. I originate from Yorkshire and this is my fifth year over here in Wales.

I began recovering from my illness at the beginning of 1994 and started writing poetry in the winter of that year. I have had four other poems published, writing under my former name of Cathie Hurcombe.

My main hobbies and interests are hill walking, photography, animals (especially dogs!) reading and writing poetry. I like to write about a variety of subjects, though it is different people in everyday life who have inspired the majority of my works.

I'd like to dedicate this poem to my mum, who works hard and plays hard! She provided the inspiration for this poem, also to Bill, who has encouraged and motivated me every step of the way.

Her Favourite Time of the Day

She'd work hard all day, till she felt she could drop
Though she'd have her set time for the duties to stop
At night she'd look forward to a good drink of sherry
The mere thought of relaxing would make her feel merry

The chores were now done, things tidied away
This was her favourite time of the day
She'd pour out a glass and light up a fag
The hard work she'd done now seemed less of a drag

The first glass was pure pleasure, it went down a treat
A few more of these, then make something to eat
Quite quickly her stresses were draining away
Who cared about money? and bills she'd to pay

There were books and the papers to read at her side
With these and a drink, in her own room she'd hide
Husband and dog packed off out for a walk
Her TV was on, or she'd phone friends and talk

She felt slightly bad about being a bit lazy
But the day's work was done and her mind was now hazy
This was her own time, only the dog to be fed
Just another glass, then away to her bed

A good sleep was needed, she now felt quite worn
She'd be back up on her feet not long after dawn
But right now her worries had all gone away
And she'd just had her favourite time of the day

Cathie Wright

Another Chance

Notes

I am R Martin, born 8th February 1929 in Nottingham. I was married to Margaret Pendleton on 30th June 1951 and we have two children, son Stephen and daughter Christine Anne. We also have two grandchildren, Matthew John and Kim Rebecca.

I have been a Justice of the Peace since 1975.

It has often been said that today
Is the first day of the rest of your life
And that's a truth that is hard to gainsay
For whatever our life has been up to now
The opportunity to make a new start
Comes to us, with the dawn of each day
But whether we take it is for us to decide
If we do, we should do so without delay
For these opportunities do not last forever
One day they are here, and then gone
And we are left to contemplate how things might have been
If we had not left so many things undone.

If only, if only, if only,
Is the plaintive cry we so often hear
From those who have missed out on their chances
And are finding life so much harder to bear
And yet, it is possible to start life anew
To rid yourself of worry and strife
If you have missed out on your chances today
Remember, tomorrow is the second day of the rest of your life.

R Martin

Notes

I am Barbara Hellewell, born 6 March 1940 in Huddersfield, West Yorkshire, a housewife/mature student. I'm married with two grown up children, Mark and Anne. At present, I am doing a home study course on poetry.

A Mother's Role is my twenty sixth poem to be published. *Supreme Guidance* published in May 1997 will be my twenty ninth poem in forty three books since starting writing in February 1994. One of my poems entitled *A Rose* written to commemorate the memory of my mother, who died in 1994, has gone into nine books, so far.

One of the books was presented to H M Queen Elizabeth, The Queen Mother, accompanied by another poem which I wrote called *Birthday Honours* for her 96th birthday, 4 August 1996.

I have gained three distinctions, the third being an Award of Excellence Certificate by Poetry Institute of the British Isles (last year renamed to Poetry in Print). Editors Choice Award Certificate by International Society of Poets plus Special Commendation Certificate by Hilton House (Publishers) Norwich. One published in local paper, also second prize in local competition (Valentine's Day).

Statement: When *Power* corrupts. *Poetry* cleanses.

This was said by John F Kennedy as part of a speech at Amhurst College (1962) and I find this very true.

A Mother's Role

A mother's role is endless
    for years and years and years.
The days of early motherhood
    bring pleasure, joy and fears.
All the different stages
    you tend with gentle care.
Seeing your offspring developing
    with ways unique and rare.

You as so very busy
Your head is in a whirl
Then everything is so complete
With a perfect boy and girl.

Oh! What bliss you are going to find
    as through the years you sail,
But as the years go quickly by
    it becomes a different tale.
Things don't go as you had planned,
    life changes with the years.
People's personalities clash
    and bring on lots of tears.

Then one day they're up and gone,
    there is no one there.
Where did all those years go,
    all those years of care?
The things that you had planned for them,
    it's not at all like that.
You are left with nothing,
    just their dog or cat.

But then, you get a 'phone call
Just when you're feeling blue
A voice says 'Hello Mum,
It's me, how are you?'

Now all those years of caring
    just melt away with pride
When you hear that voice say
    'It's me Mum'
Your heart swells with *love* inside.

Barbara Hellewell

Notes

Last year I was fortunate enough to have my first poem published in the first edition of Mists of Time, entitled *Life is Like a Mountain*.

This poem was dedicated to my Grandfather who would have been very proud, but, unfortunately, he died suddenly before the publication was issued. However, his memory will always live on in my heart, and therefore I would like to dedicate this poem to him also, remembering fond times we spent together.

My Grandfather loved life, and he told me that each morning when he woke up that he looked at the sky, at the beauty of the land, and realised just how lucky he was to be here.

This poem is about wanting to be someone special, but in reality everyone is special, in their own way.

My Grandfather was very special to me.

How I Long!

How I long, one day
to be a budding swan
And float with dignity
As shining stars do hang

I long to be a beauty
in the middle of a war
like a rosebud
in a mass of graves

I long to be the rising sun
At dawn where lovers sit
like an eternal warmth
to their ever growing love

I long to be a good deed
A hero at the rescue
When someone's struggling to survive
like a candle does for light

How I long and wonder
If life was meant to be
Just the way it always has
like me being me

Alison Crane (17)

Notes

I live in Portrush in Northern Ireland, right on the Atlantic Ocean coast. We have wonderful natural scenery here. You can guess all my poems are about nature and the sea. My poem *Grey Waters* is about all the different moods of the sea, and my love of the sea and nature and home.

I have been writing poetry for many years. It was my mother who inspired me to write poetry. I have a number of poems published in anthologies. Our family is musical, my mother was a music teacher, and so was I. My brother was a DMus. I think that poetry and music go together.

I am a retired pensioner so I have plenty of time to write poetry.

Grey Waters

Grey waters dreaming all the while
Grey waters over many a mile
I'd roam with you all day
And never stray

Grey waters curling round my shore
Grey waters I love you more and more
And I must go my love to show

Grey waters what are you tonight?
Grey waters just a misty light
Of silver shining out to me
Oh my grey sea

Grey waters mirror of God's sky
Grey waters how my soul flies
To be with you alone
My own dear home

Stella Brown

Night Feed

Notes

My name is Brenda. I am 48 years old, I have been married for 29 years and have 3 grown up children: 2 sons , aged 28 and 16 and my daughter who is 25.

I live in Chingford, which is in East London, and I work as a mid-day assistant in White-hall Primary School.

My hobbies are: reading, writing and watching good films, also I am learning very basic sign language at my school and I thoroughly enjoy this.

I have been writing poetry for as long as I can remember, but I usually only write for family and friends, sort of, personalised humorous poems which reflect everyday incidents in their lives. The main intention being, to hopefully, cheer them up,. and *Dunblane* is probably the most serious poem that I have ever written.

It's 3am I'm wide awake,
    Something disturbed my sleep,
I stretch my limbs, stifle a yawn,
    Then, from my bed I leap.

I look around, I listen,
    But nothing I hear or see,
Besides the ticking of the clock,
    Could possibly waken me.

But my slumber has been broken,
    In the middle of the night,
And I must find out, by whom or what?
    I reach out for the light.

I'm blinded for a moment,
    As darkness is no more,
Then there it is, a tiny sound,
    I heard it, that's for sure.

I hold my breath, I dare not move,
    My heart is beating fast,
Then suddenly the sound, but louder this time,
    And the moment of fear is past.

I start to laugh, I can't believe,
    That I can be so dumb,
I completely forgot that four days ago,
    I became a brand new mum -

And the noise which now is loud and clear,
    Is my brand new bundle of joy,
Letting me know, it's time to feed,
    My beautiful baby boy.

Brenda Barker

The Rat Race

Notes

I'm seventy three and went to an elementary school, leaving when I was fourteen. Whilst at school I entered a poetry writing competition, although I had never written poetry before. I won it and another competition before I left school. My headmaster told me that I must always write, but I didn't compose any more poetry until I went overseas in the army during the war. I didn't do any more writing until I got married at twenty seven, then I couldn't stop! That lasted a number of years but these days I really have to be inspired before I lift pen to paper.

I am a retired painter and decorator, I have three sons, three grandchildren and live in Derby where I was brought up. I've had several poems published which has been good for my ego, but never brought any monetary gain!

I've been a Derby County fanatic since I 'went to the match' at the age of six with my dad.

I would like to dedicate this poem to my dear wife, Gwen, who was taken from me on December 24th 1995. She loved all animals, especially dogs.

He had an eye for business, he'd felt that all along,
When he joined the self-employed, not a thing went wrong;
He'd always been a painter, no snag to him was new,
He used his vast experience, and his business quickly grew.

Customers would tell their friends, and soon the time came, when
He had a thriving enterprise, and employed a dozen men;
But with success the worries came, insurance and VAT,
He rarely had a good night's sleep, bleary eyes could hardly see.

But still the work kept rolling in, until he cried 'Enough,
I'm getting out of this rat race, this life is much too tough;'
So he sold up everything he owned, his house and business went,
He took his wife to live in peace, a retired country gent.

He bought a dog, a pedigree bitch, if you'll pardon the expression,
His friend's dog, of the self same breed, had a mating session,
This canine match produced ten pups, each sold for fifty pounds,
He found that he was hooked again, but this time breeding hounds.

He couldn't stop, the business grew, he bought another whelp,
He started his own kennels, but this meant hiring help;
He had a thriving business and employed a dozen men,
With forms to fill and VAT it's the rat race once again.

So, if you feel like opting out, just bear this in mind,
We cannot change the way we're made, we just need to unwind;
If you're not happy in your work and you're no longer keen,
Don't rush to change your patch of grass, this side's just as green.

Ken Burrows

Notes

For Mam and Uncle Bert. If
just one person remembers
you after you have gone, then
you really haven't gone at all.

Remembered always.

Dedicated to Allan, my lord
and mentor, thanks for your
support.

Eternally Yours

When my time
has come and gone
memories of me
will linger on.
No tears for me,
no crying in the
graveyard mists
for in your thoughts
I'll still exist.
Remember me for
who I am and not
for what I've done
remember me and
where I've gone,
and then I'll live on and on.

San

Notes

Originally from Berkshire, having moved to Derbyshire 30 years ago. Being a mother of four children, it's only now that I have time and am able to pursue my interests in local history, walking and wildlife.

This is my fifth poem published since I started writing a year ago.

I would like to dedicate this poem to my children, Sharon, Louise, Kirk and Scott.

Cressbrook Dale

This quiet dale that I walk in silence
all green and sides so steep,

I hear nothing except the fleeing clouds
and the bleating of the sheep,

There might only be me alive today
there is not the smallest sound,

And so I march on, so quiet of foot
for 'Peter's Stone' I'm bound,

To see the bloodthirsty work of days gone by
of gibbets and men put in chains,

On that rock so solidly standing there
ignoring the sun and the rain,

That once had ravens flying high over its granite face,
But were extinguished long ago by men of the human race,

In that dale, I climbed the rock, of
legends of long ago

And felt the presence of men, who'd never, ever know

Of those few sunny hours I spent, walking and
climbing with glee,

In Ravensdale, the legend's name, for the
place I had come to see.

Sonia Jameson

Notes

I was born in Clacton-on-Sea on the Essex coast, on the 5th of May 1958, into a family of seven brothers and eight sisters who are all older than me with the exception of one sister.

I have two children, Robert aged 15 years and Charlene aged 13 years. I am a painter and decorator by occupation. I enjoy working with my hands and find relaxation making decorative eggs from goose egg shells. I can spend hours on this delicate and challenging hobby.

It was during a stay in hospital, about two and a half years ago in 1994, that I began writing poetry to pass the time. Since then I have written poems whenever something inspires me to. I enjoy the peace and tranquillity of the countryside, which is where *Twilight* was inspired.

Sugar and Spice

Sugar and Spice were two little mice who lived in a bonny wee house
It was so very small you'd hardly see it at all being just big enough
for a mouse.
It was cosy within and meat as a pin with everything shining and clean
For such a good housewife was that little mouse-wife she kept her home
fit for a queen.
Now Sugar and Spice had twin baby mice, sweet William and Marigold
May
No happier pair would you find anywhere if you searched for a year and a
day.
One day mother mouse was spring cleaning her house while the little ones
played in the sun, when a friendly elf came, saying . . . Teazle's my name
Oh please let me join in the fun.
Of course you shall play said Marigold May for such a kind mouse was she
They played game after game and good pals they became
'Til mother mouse called . . . time for tea.
Then the newcomer sighed, 'I'm so lonely,' he cried and looked so sad, that
little elf.
I've got no father or mother nor sister or brother and so I live by myself.
Then Sugar and Spice those soft hearted mice just could not send him
away.
But their house was so small there was no room at all so where oh where
could he stay.
Then kind father mouse built him a house next door to their own
Where Teazle could stay and see them each day and never feel alone.
How Teazle's eyes gleamed he had never dreamed that a cottage so pretty
and trim
With windows so bright and walls shining white would ever belong to him.
And now side by side so happy they bide yet no one would guess they were
there.
So if you should go where the wild poppies grow.
You just might see them there.

Bradley Symes

Notes

I was born in Hartlepool, Cleveland, on the 16th December 1962. I have an older brother, Stewart, who is married to Angela, and a new nephew called Daniel Stewart. I have a younger brother called Scott and a younger sister called Vicky. I am married to Ronnie and we have a son, Carl, who is fifteen and a daughter, Sarah Kay, who is eleven.

I have been fortunate enough to have had three poems published entitled, *Diabetes, Insomnia* and *Land of Dreams*. I had *Witches Eve* and *Every Dog has its Day*, printed in our local newspaper, The Hartlepool Mail, and I received an Editor's Choice Award for outstanding achievement in poetry presented by The International Library of Poetry.

I like listening to grunge bands, Nirvana and Hole and follow the Seattle Super Sonic's basketball games on television.

Inspiration for my poetry derives from my own personal thoughts, feelings and experiences.

Lost

Something inside me's been lost by the way,
I only feel emptiness, day after day,
time passes slowly, dragging its heels,
ticking and tocking, turning its wheels.

What can I do, where can I go?
Suspended in limbo, an all time low,
my feelings have troubled me, I just want to scream,
I keep hoping I'll wake from this terrible dream.

Sometimes my head feels like its going to explode,
who will listen to me, to help me unload?
The worries, the anguish, the hurt and the pain,
gnawing inside me, again and again.

Would I sell my soul to the devil, if all this would go?
Definitely, yes, I'm feeling that low,
what I wouldn't give to be happy and carefree,
to leave this depression, and once again, become me.

Wendy Bage

Resolution Day

Each year there comes a parting,
Yet we're not sad at all,
In fact we are so happy,
we even have a ball,
Tho' it's winter we make merry,
whilst happy songs we sing,
For we never see the leaving,
or hear the next one coming in,
Now, departing hour is drawing nigh,
so we stand and raise our glasses high,
without a sound, the old year's gone,
'Auld Lang Syne' is now the song,
Church bells peal, their message clear,
To one and all 'a glad new year,'
Without a tear we've said 'farewell'
To what has gone before,
Look forward to the future year,
with hope for peace the whole world o'er.

May Dabrowiecki

Notes

I am 60 years of age, I have four daughters and seven grandchildren, all of whom I love beyond words. I served 25 years in the army, I live and work in Colchester for the MOD.

I have had several poems published by 'Poetry Now' over the past two years.

My interest are my family, reading, military history, sports and country music.

I would like to dedicate this poem to my grandchildren.

The Countryside

What became of the endless fields,
of golden buttercups,
have the bulldozers,
covered them all up.

What became of the butterflies,
winging on the breeze,
are they missing,
all the chopped down trees.

Where is the countryside,
rolling hills, with flowing streams,
has it gone for ever,
was it all a dream?

What became of the beauty,
the landscape, I used to see,
is this the poor years,
is this, nature's poverty?

Brian Morris

Grandchild Coming

Notes

I am a middle aged housewife named Joan married to John, we have three boys, David, Christopher and Mark. We also have two grandchildren, Andrew and Aimèe.

I have had eight other poems printed. I started writing about 30 years ago, but stopped until now. I never thought about having any printed.

Happenings in life inspire me to write them. This poem came to me as I was waiting for my granddaughter to be born. I also love nature and walking.

I would like to dedicate this poem to my granddaughter Aimèe.

I'm so happy, I'm so glad,
I feel so tense and tight
But, also, I feel so sad.
My grandchild has begun the fight.

Future Grandma's and Grandad's,
Sit very close to the phone
Wondering whether girl or lad,
Will it stay or will it roam.

Husband phone's his mum.
Wishing she was closer by.
He will be glad when it's all done
Wanting a very good cry.

A lot of advice from the old,
But, really, you're on your own
But now, the story is beginning to unfold.
As baby slips into the world.
Everyone *must be told.*

J M Lerigo

Notes

The English language has always been a great delight to me, especially that of light verse. I would often jot down a few words for fun, but, as I never considered them any good, never tried to get any published. Most of it was of a humorous nature, about everyday life. My career which was nursing, often featured.

When I retired in 1979 I did intend to at least try. Instead I chose to concentrate on painting.

However, last Christmas I was strongly advised to turn to something which I would be able to handle more easily. I did and found poetry to be the answer. About that time an advert appeared in our local paper encouraging new writers to try. I did but certainly didn't expect a reply. Imagine my surprise when one came! Then a local friend gave me your address and suggested I try. This of course fired my enthusiasm.

Happiness

When you are young you wonder why,
Happiness appears to pass you by.
You've yet to learn - at a later date,
That a grumpy soul is what most folk hate.

Happiness starts when one is very young,
Then most of your years are filled with fun,
At times you feel very weary,
But pleasant thoughts will always keep you cheery.

In the early years you may feel left out,
But later you learn what life is all about.
Pleasant people are usually sought after,
That arduous task is made much lighter with laughter.

As you age many lines may appear,
But often they are of cheer.
So don't be downhearted for you see,
Many are there because of glee.

Although your road may be very tough,
Those inner glows help you through the rough.
Happiness you'll always find,
Can help to achieve that peace of mind.

Again a smile and a bright word could help another along,
And will often herald a pretty song
So instead of always fearing the worst,
Let those bubbles of joy arise and burst.

Betty E Green

Notes

My name is Gay Jones, I am forty-five, single and have no children. I was born in Mountain Ash in South Wales, although I now live in Leicester.

I have written poetry for many years but until recently never submitted any for publication. I have had one poem published in *Mists of Time* by poetry today called *Shaun*.

Most of my poetry comes from my own life experience. My favourite poet is Ella Wheeler Wilcox, I was introduced to her by a friend, now sadly deceased.

I would like to dedicate this second achievement to 'Sandie'.

The Familiar Stranger

Millions of meaningless words, hours of endless chat
All concerned with you, the weather, this or that
But you never really listen to anything I say
It stops you facing up to *it* until another day.

I understand your need to keep the pain away
But it hasn't left you know, it's only held at bay
You remind me of a dam straining to keep back the flood
What will happen when it cracks and the pain is there for good?

This pain so sharp, in seconds, it engulfs you all entire
And every thought you think adds fuel to its fire
Questions by the hundreds all without an answer
Waiting there to kill you, growing like a cancer.

Could *you* have contained these feelings for thirty years or more
I am your daughter, didn't you notice my pain oozing out of each pore
If not, why not, I have the script but not the plot
I didn't ask to be alive and that's exactly what I got.

G Jones

Notes

I am 36, a single parent to a daughter of eight years and live in Basingstoke.

I have had poetry published in the Basingstoke Gazette and in the Cat Protection League Newsletter.

My interests include gardening, working on a voluntary basis for the Cat Protection League, writing, environmental issues.

This poem was written after observing my cats, of which I now have three. I am cat crazy and find they are wonderful and loving companions. I also do a lot of voluntary work for the Cat Protection League and this poem has been published in their newsletter. It is dedicated to Smouhe, Ziggy and Poppy who have given me such love over the years.

Who Me?

I love to sit and stare at shadows on the wall,
to smell the rug, to chase a bug,
oh! Life is such a ball.

I love the way the sun makes little ponds of light,
as it reflects through the window
oh! What a pleasing sight.

On the bed, on the floor, and on the windowsill,
little ponds of happiness,
oh! Life is such a thrill.

To laze and gaze lethargically and watch the
world go by,
to eat and drink is my favourite, I think,
and then to slumber for a while.

You may think that it's a strange life
at that,
but then again you see, it's not, if you're a cat.

Carol Walker

Notes

My name is Marion Stevens and I have been married to Percy for 32 years. We have a lovely cat called Poppett.

I am 52 years old and have worked for 25 years as an office worker. For the last five years I have been a care assistant in a residential home called Tudor Lodge in Torquay. My hobbies include astronomy and writing.

I have been writing poetry for the past 10 years and have had the following published:
Ethiopia in Poetry Now Regional Anthology, *Hope* in Life's Like That by Anchor Books, *Friendship* in Christian Poets From The West Country by Triumph House. I have a poem to be published in the autumn by The International Society of Poets called *You* in an anthology called *A Lasting Calm.*

How not to be an Amateur Astronomer

I didn't realise thee would be a storm,
Never mind, I am wrapped up nice and warm.
As it set off with my 'scope tonight
I hope to see Halley's comet in flight
This hill's rather steep, I'll stop for a break
I wish I had remembered to bring some cake,
I'm hungry and cold now, but I must get to the top,
If I want to see the comet, I really must not stop.
Now let's set up the telescope, O dear I forgot the stand,
I'll just have to hope I've got a steady hand,
Now it's started to rain, I forgot my boots leak,
As I walk about they have started to squeak,
It's gone all cloudy now, I can't even see,
Is there another amateur astronomer as silly as me?
I'll check my book, O dear is that the date,
To see Halley's comet, it's much too late,
Never mind, to climb this hill in the wet and cold,
To see the sights of the heaven's is a wonder to behold,
Next time I'll choose a nice dry night,
Perhaps I'll see another comet in flight,
To be an astronomer takes patience and time,
This is the end of this silly rhyme.

Marion Stevens

Notes

Born in 1934 and married to
Trevor Hunt. I am a housewife and mother with four
children: Christopher, Jeffrey,
Jeniffer and Jacqueline. I have
six grandchildren and one
great-grandchild.

I live in a flat and love to do
my garden, keep fit and
walking.

This earth and all its beauty
are free to us all but we all
take so much for granted.
Life itself is there for you and
me.

Beauty

The sky at night
Is a wondrous sight
And so is the sun
Through the day.
The snow that falls on
A frosty night
And quickly blows away.
The trees so tall,
The sky so blue
A rainbow in the sky.
The sea so deep
The sand so still
We are born
But alas we must die.
These things of beauty
Will be last till the
End of time.

D Hunt

Notes

Born in Kenya (East Africa) 61 years ago. Lived in Dinas Powys near Cardiff for 32 years. Now widowed, with one daughter aged 27 years in USA.

I only started writing poetry a year ago and have had three poems accepted by the International Library of Poetry, already printed in three anthologies. I have had three more accepted including: *Goodbye Wimbledon* which was printed last year by Penhaligon Page.

My hobbies are reading, theatre, travelling, out-doors and wildlife.

Certain experiences and events have inspired me to capture them in verse.

I hope this poem will give others hope and encouragement towards positive attitudes.

Come, Tell Me

Come, whisper, tell me
Person of mystery, what worries thee?
What weight of burden do you bear
Why so sad, tell me, I care?
Life is not so bad
Together we'll try to make you glad
Unload, unwind, forget sad things
Soon you'll be flying high on wings
A bright new tomorrow is in store for you
I feel it, I wish it and I'll pray for you

Joyce Roberts

Rock'n'Roll

'What's that song you're singing dad? What do you call it rock and roll
dad? Bootlace tie and creeper soles, drainpipe trousers and winkle picker
shoes, were you in the war dad? It sounds so old dad.' 'Careful son you
don't know what you're saying, no one sits still when Little Richard's playing, Elvis Presley he was the best, Big Bopper sang 'Chantilly Lace,' Jerry
Lee Lewis played standing on a piano and 'did you know George Formby
dad, didn't he play a banjo?' 'He played ukulele son during the war, before
my time, that was a bore. When rock and roll came around it shook the
world, what a sound.' 'Michael Jackson he's the best dad, the music now
leaves rock and roll for dead dad, we have house, garage, dance and rap,
that rock and roll is nothing but c--p.' 'That's enough son off to bed and let
me get dressed like a ted.'

Tony Neesham

My Family

Notes

I live in Oswestry, and have been married to John for 31 years. We've got three sons, one daughter, one daughter-in-law, and two granddaughters. Andrew and Sharon, with little Gemma and Nicola, David, Mark and Sarah. Mark and Sarah are still living at home with us, which I love. My family and friends mean everything to me. They are what inspires me to write, which is why I wrote *My Family*.

I like to write about things that I enjoy, and things that have actually happened. I love having fun, and enjoy life in general. So there's always plenty to write about.

I find writing poetry most relaxing. I started a while back now, when I worked part-time in a local school. Every time anyone left, I would write a verse in their card, and it went on from there. I now work full-time in a nursing home, which I also enjoy, but I still find the time to write.

The important things in my life, are my family, and friends.
To be content and happy with them, until my life on earth ends.
There's been so many happy times, in my life.
From growing up, and meeting John, to then become his wife.

Two years on, along came our first little boy.
This filled us with such happiness, and brought us so much joy.
Soon then we had our second son to keep him company.
Now instead, of one, I've two upon my knee.

The first was Andrew, the second Dave, with a head of tiny curls.
One more, would just complete the boys, and then we'd have some girls.
Our third son arrived at one minute past twelve on the 19th July
We decided to call him Mark Anthony. Even though I don't know why?
Their dad taught them all to swim, and soon, they loved the water,
I think it's nearly time, we have our little baby daughter.

When Chris, my friend, visited our house. The cat decided to
Catch a mouse. I knew it was time for our baby to arrive, as
Chris shouted out, 'It's still alive.'
I said, 'Don't worry he'll let it go,' as she climbed upon the chair.
An hour later our daughter arrived, with a mass of dark brown hair.
John was so pleased, he had stopped with me, to see our daughter arrive.
I think that completes our family, I don't think we'll make it five.

Joyce Jones

Notes

I am aged 54 years and a housewife. I have two grown up children.

I am a great romantic, and daydreamer, that's when my composing comes to mind. I have been composing poetry for about two years but have never entered my poetry in any competition.

My hobbies are: flower arranging, reading good fiction novels and any form of artwork.

My poetry started when I composed a poem for my dear mum and then suddenly grew from that day onwards.

Mother

Mothers are, heartfelt love and beyond
As life ascends, goes on , and goes on,
Yesterday's tears we like to forget,
Alas with just a little regret.

My thoughts roll on by with fluffy clouds in the sky
Of you my dear Mama
Here in my heart they lie.
Thoughts of unending flowers from here and below
Remind of Mama's unending love that's what you show.

Avril Weller

Step by Step

Notes

Hello, my name is Pauline Warren. I was born in May 1947 and I live in Croydon, Surrey, with my watercolourist husband Les and our thoroughly spoilt cat Mazie.

I have been interested (in an ever increasing way) in different forms of rhyme/verse/poetry all my life, from those I knew as a child to those that have come my way since childhood; and sources other than the obvious - nursery rhymes, poetry books, songs and hymns - such as the uniquely special language of the authorised (King James) version of the Holy Bible, God's amazing abundance and diversity in nature and a wide variety of instrumental music, together with all the usual day by day occurrences, have also played their part in stirring and evoking thoughts and experiences to more and more frequently put poetically on paper.

It is only quite recently, however, that I have been persuaded to share any of my poetical attempts with a wider audience than friends and family, and I was delighted when for the first time last year (1996) I had two poems published in books, one in *The Other Side of the Mirror* and another in *Mists of Time*. Now I am here!

There's such a lot that one should do,
    and more one feels one must!
Besides the things one dreams of,
    sighing: 'Oh, if only - if just . . .'

But there is where the danger lies,
    in allowing oneself to believe
it's because of so-and-so and such-and-such
    that one's unable to achieve.

And the answer? Quiet, firm resolve
    to take all a step at a time!
To be pleased with the one step just taken
    and not bemoan it wasn't eight or nine!

But more, much more importantly
    is to ask God to be near in our pacing,
then thank Him for every step's progress made
    and each future step we hope also to be taking.

P M Warren

Kathleen's Epitaph

Notes

My name is Kathleen Patricia
Peebles, I was born 2nd November 1940 in Stratford-
upon-Avon. My home is in
the village of Leek Wootton.
Leek Wootton is between
Kenilworth and Warwick.

I have had twenty poems
published. Royalties are paid
to most of my poems, I love
writing poetry.

Hobbies are gardening and of
course poetry.

I started writing poetry in
1994. *My Dream* was my
first poem to be published.
Life inspires me to write poetry, subjects are never ending. To keep writing poetry I
hope I do and give lots of
enjoyment - especially for
you.

When I have gone to the world unknown,
To see loved ones and friends dear -
I shall be happy, not filled with fear
My life fulfilled in every way
I know I shall never be alone,
People will say, she was a good'n
Always there to help each day
And always there to pay her way!
My name will live on, with the poem's I love
Perhaps I should write for Him above,
Keep in His good books
For my life ahead,
Still write my poems I hope I can
I must be my biggest fan!
So through those gates I shall go
Note paper and pen in hand
And raring to have a go -
In the unknown my poems will be read
She's a good'n will be said

Kathleen Patricia Peebles

Freedom of Spirit

Notes

Lorraine 'J J' Bush was born
in Slough. She has two children, is single and is currently living in Sidmouth,
Devon.

She has been seriously writing poetry since 1984. Her
writing covers many aspects
of life, usually written from
personal experiences.

Her inspiration for Freedom
of Spirit was found by
watching the sea and her
own imagination of what it
would be like to be free from
the chaos of our world.

Cast your eyes, upon the exorbitant sea,
Mortality taking over me.
I gaze, upon the ocean's edge,
Reveals to me, its haunting quest.

I wait, and watch, with childish glee,
For the waves of spirit, to enliven me.
For some comfort, of my weary brow,
To douse, the drudge and hell somehow.

The immortal gods, they lift me up,
And feed to me, elixir's cup.
Of life and freedom, they can expose,
Sweet gift, of life's enchanted rose.

I find myself, there, wading in,
White waves encase me, prevail, and win.
My death was efficient, and painlessly still,
I succumb, to the God's inevitable will.

Then a mystical encounter, raced over me,
An electrifying jolt, seared through the sea.
I emerged, a beautiful dolphin rare,
And my grief, dispersed, into the air.

I embraced the Gods, in the glittering sea,
And submerged, triumphant, my spirit set free.
My brothers, emerged in their numbers extreme,
The most wondrous sight, I had ever seen.
They beckoned sweetly, embracing me
And we disappeared, in the vast, blue sea.

L 'JJ' Bush

Notes

My age is - above God's allotted time, yet young in heart and spirit. I am married to Susan (forty-something) and have one son, Anderson, who is 21 and a daughter, Saleika, 18.

Rudyard Kipling's poem *If* impressed and inspired me long years ago; since then, many poets past and present have kept my love of reading and writing poetry alive.

Poetry to my mind is the voice and soul of the people expressing their thoughts, their hopes, dreams, their love, joys, aspirations, concerns and even, at times, their despair.

People and nature inspire my writings, subjects which give the poet unlimited scope and thus enabling the poet to have an affinity with the reader in easily understood writing.

Ambition? Well, it's a little late for that, albeit Poet Laureate would be a desirable honour, most poets I'm sure would agree! I'd rather aspire to being a poet with a million readers than a millionaire with just one reader.

My poems *Homo Sapien* (Poetry Today), *Mists of Time* (Hardback) and *Corn Fantasy* (Poet's Chorus in paperback, by Anchor Books) are just two of many other diverse poems I have written and hope to eventually have published.

The Silent Friend was written in answer to my wife and daughter's repeated question, whilst looking in the mirror, do I look alright?

The Silent Friend

As you look in a mirror what do you see?
Maybe the image pleases albeit you may disagree
Yet the point about a mirror is it tells you what you need
It speaks the truth regardless, a genuine friend indeed.

It doesn't shout or raise a voice it just reflects your image
It doesn't even belittle you or insult your looks or carriage
It is your silent servant and you alone can make it glow
You look in it, it tells you all you want to know.

Love it or hate it, it is your silent friend
Remaining aloof till needed and faithful to the end
A silent shining mirror responding to your every call
Whether carried with you personally or just hanging on a wall.

Scorcher

My Sister

Notes

I am married with two sons and five grandchildren. I have always enjoyed writing, but until I retired had never submitted my work for publication. Since which time, I have had numerous poems and articles published.

The subject of my poems covers a wide spectrum, but I prefer to write in a similar vein to Patience Strong. Inspiration for my poetry comes from events both personal and world, people I meet, places I visit, in fact anything that comes to mind.

My hobbies are cooking, reading, crossword puzzles, dancing, and I am an avid cricket fan.

Many years of love and kinship we have shared,
Life has been more bearable knowing that you cared.
Together we've cried through periods of rain,
And wiped away the tears when the sun shone again.
Precious memories we have locked within our hearts,
Memories of loved ones with whom we've had to part.
Memories of bygone days, both miserable and fair,
Episodes of family life, no one else can share.
We have one friend however, who never leaves our side,
Lord Jesus Christ - our Saviour and our Guide.
Whatever fate befalls us, good fortune or adversity,
All is woven in the threads of His great tapestry.
In the quiet of my room at night, when my work is through,
I thank the Lord for sending me a sister such as *you*.

Annelyn Jax

Notes

I am 95 years old, I walk with a zimmer frame after falling three times and having had operations on my hips.

Since June of this year, I am now living in Durham with my daughter, a widow like me. She is a nurse. I taught English in several schools, my favourite subject, and poetry especially. My poems have been accepted by Anchor Books and Poetry Today, and also in Woman's Weekly.

Wherever I Stray is the outcome of my mongrel dog, Vic, my loyal partner during my widowhood.

A Smile

I'm old, very old. I've passed the years
Allotted to me, of three score and ten.
I'm told I live on borrowed time, because
I'm ninety five. As I live I pay my way
And every day I try to give something to cheer.

It may be a smile, 'that costs nothing' you say,
Yet it's a way of helping another
Maybe a brother to face a fate worse than death
He feels alone, deserted and sad,
Whatever the cost a smile isn't lost.

Just pass it on and you've paid back,
And it grows into a grin,
And it isn't a sin to shout good cheer
When anyone's near to hear you.

And the day's work is over,
Quicker and lighter.
All for a smile, one to another
And it makes the day much brighter.

Doris White

Little Me

There once was a little girl,
who had a secret magic spell,
she only had one you see
one spell was enough for little me
little me was only seven
she dreamed of going up to heaven
to see the angels and their golden wings
and hear their sweet voices sing

Oh little me had high hopes
while she played with her skipping ropes
she told Grandpa Joe how she'd go to heaven
but Grandpa Joe just laughed
he thought little me was a bit daft
on one hot sunny day in mid-June
Grandpa Joe went to little me's room
but she was nowhere to be seen
except for the note by the washing machine

I've gone now Grandpa Joe
like I said so, to see the angels and their
golden wings
I've gone to heaven and so you see
my magic spell worked for me.

Alyson Silver

Waiting in Line

Notes

E Sheldon is 45 years old and works as a dustman. He has been writing on and off since he was 16 and hopes that people will get joy from his work.

My tea's so hot as it hits my lips,
Still feeling bad from last night,
Must soon make a move
To put on some clothes,
And rush on my way to work.

Work today could go away
Oh really if only it could
But don't think that
Cause you're feeling bad
Cause someone could soon take your place.

You know there are many
Who have no work
Would love to be like you
They're just there
To jump and take your place.

E Sheldon

Our Father's Way

Notes

My name is Dorothy Carey and I was born in Cardonagh, Co Donegal, my parents are Robert and Edith Henderson. I am married to Lexie Carey and have two children, Garry aged seventeen and Sharon aged fourteen. I am a housewife and also run a small business.

At the end of my education I obtained a Leaving Certificate at Secondary Level and am currently undertaking studies in Creative Writing.

My hobbies are reading, writing and picture framing.

I have four poems published.

This poem, *Our Father's Way*, was written after the death of my father.

The title refers to our Heavenly Father, and the poem portrays His plan for our lives.

As I saw the calmness and stillness of the deceased, grief was overshadowed by reassurance that God knows when to call the weary home, and acceptance, that death is part of life.

I talk to you, and hold, your hand
As friend and brother round you stand
Your transient smile hides doubt and fear
Our lives you always tried to cheer

But in your eyes, I see your pain
And in my heart, I feel the same
Bewildered, baffled, not quite sure
If we are meant to find a cure

Then with that breath, and final sigh
You closed your eyes, I'll ask not why
For God alone, knows all too well
When He must toll the final bell

We sat in silence, calm and still
Our last goodbyes, let teardrops spill
But you looked peaceful, free of pain
How could we wish you back again?

Now months have turned to weeks of years
Time heals the wounds, and dries the tears
Leaves memories wedged in solemn days
Acceptance of our Father's ways.

Dorothy Carey

Notes

Kathleen Stringer is a mother of four children, grandmother of four boys and one girl. She is a retired administration clerk who worked at the Sheffield Magistrates' Court for a number of years, in the family proceedings department.

She is a born-again Christian in her early fifties, who writes children's stories and poetry.

Having had two poems published in 1996, she is hoping that this poem is one of many to be published in 1997.

Growing Old

The passing years have drifted by
Gone are the days and the babies' cry.
With memories of sunny days and picnic bliss.
The singing birds and the stolen kiss.

Here are the years of the falling leaves.
Buttoned up shirt with tight fitted sleeves.
Colourless hair and wrinkled neck.
And now that kiss, a quick little peck.

Past are the days, they've gone for good.
When you could have loved deeper - you know that you should
There's still just a chance to fill that gap,
When you wondered off the heavenly map.

Age doesn't matter - time doesn't wait.
Take stock of your years, before it's too late.
Don't give a frown, instead give a smile
May be you're living along your last mile.

Kathleen Stringer

Over the Sea

Notes

Andrew Condon is aged 42; his parents are Florrie and Martin Condon. He has 2 sisters and 3 brothers. At present, he is unemployed and lives in London.

He started writing in November 1991, coming up with a short story called *Winnie*.

Over the Sea is dedicated to Theresa Renzi and Susanne Ramstedt.

There's a woman, who comes from over the sea,
She brings her love to me, to me her love she
Brings and, it breaks my heart, to see her go,
Back over the sea.

She's as sweet as honey, as honey is sweet, she
Brings her sweet love to me, to me she brings her
Sweet love and, it breaks my heart to see her go,
Back over the sea.

She's the only one, who holds my heart within her
Hands, in her hands, my heart she holds, for now
And for evermore and, it breaks my heart, to see
Her go, back over the sea.

She's as warm, as a summer's day, so warm you just
Dream the day way, within her arms, on a summer's
Day and, it breaks my heart, to see her go,
Back over the sea.

And, it breaks my heart, to see her leave, to go
Back over the sea, back over the sea she goes.

Andrew Condon

Notes

I was born in Leicester,. 27 August 1952. My interests are: astronomy, transport (especially railways, vintage buses, trams, aircraft), travel, walking (coast, mountains, etc), people and places (geography), wildlife, especially lepidoptery (butterflies and moths), ornithology, botany and para-psychology.

Various things inspire me to express my feelings in poetry, especially wild and beautiful places, but I sometimes get ideas of various kinds and I occasionally feel the need to write down some of these thoughts.

It is then largely a matter of getting the poetry to rhyme (I always make either the 2nd and 4th successive lines rhyme or else the 1st/2nd, 3rd/4th, etc): it is also important to get roughly the same number of syllables per line. so that the poetry 'flows' when read.

That is just about all there is basically; I don't have any particular format or theme, I just write what I feel, sometimes putting myself in the position of another person, either living or fictional, but I always have to be aware of a strong visual image of the people or places about which I write.

Insomnia

The hour is close to midnight
So guard your children well
He stalks the moors by moonlight
With thirteen hounds from hell
And when he sees the little house
Asleep inside its glade
He craves to feed on mortal flesh
And sharpens up his blade
Cadaver eyes glare cruelly
From a face deformed by hate
He knows that once the lights go out
He won't have long to wait.

The child awakes from fitful sleep
In deepest, darkest night
Is that the wind that howls outside?
He cowers down in fright
But soon the boy confronts his fears
His mind is more at ease
He always gets disturbing dreams
When he eats too much cheese!
He's wide awake and cannot sleep
So he jumps out of bed
Goes out to see his two pet mice
Down by the garden shed.

The world awakes to misty dawn
A mother's cries are heard
Her precious son has disappeared
Gone off without a word
No trace of him was ever found
Though many tried to help
But on a dark and dismal night
Folk sometimes hear the yelp
Of some pathetic tortured soul
Cut off from those he loved
A hapless child forever doomed
To feast on human blood.

M J King

The Dreamer

Notes

I wrote the poem The
Dreamer because if I have a
problem or the weather isn't
too bad I like to go for a nice
long walk. It doesn't cost you
anything, it's good for your
health and you see a lot more
than you would from a window of a car.

Sometimes I can get lost in
my thoughts, but it is nice for
a moment to escape from the
stresses and strains of everyday life and imagine that you
are somewhere else, some-
where really nice.

When it rains I sometimes
pull down my umbrella
around me to shut everyone
out and imagine myself sitting beside a nice cosy log
fire.

Well I can dream can't I?

I'm a dreamer can't you tell, I walk past people I know well
They call to me but I can't see them, I'm far away in some green glen
Off into a lovely dream, standing by a sparkling stream
Beautiful sky and golden sun, this lovely dream has just begun
Then the heavens open wide, the rain pours down, the wind blows wild
Down I come back to the earth and hurry home for all it's worth
And sit beside a cosy fire, till I drift, my mind climbs higher
Off into a lovely dream, standing by a sparkling stream

Susan Milburn

Why?

It is 3 o'clock in the morning
Why can't I go to sleep?
In a few more hours 'twill be dawning
And the birds will begin to cheep.

I was so tired and weary
And needed a good nights' rest
So came to bed nice and early
And tried my very best.

Counting sheep by the hundred
And closing my eyes so tight;
I've tossed and turned in my cosy bed
But still cannot sleep tonight.

I spent a while with my book
And had a drink of Ovaltine
My pillows I punched and shook
And snuggled in sheets cool and clean.

Not having to go to work is a boon
For I would never keep awake.
At home, I can snooze in the afternoon
And have a long 'tea break.'

If, by chance, I go to sleep after all
I won't wake up till about ten
I don't need a morning call
So I can just go to sleep again.

H M Beresford

Short Stop

Notes

I was blissfully sitting on a
train bound for Leicester
when I started to write a
lengthy poem about my love
of trains, out of this poem
came this shortened version
which often happens and is
one of the joys of writing
poetry.

To write about
A train
without sounding naff
Put it down
if your bored
I won't be annoyed
In fact
I don't think
I can do it.
So here's where it stops
we're at the station
Everyone off!

Barbara Boyer

The Patient's Lament

Notes

I am a 49 year old grand-mother, I have a son of 24 and a daughter of 28 (the mother of my four grand-children). I have lived in St Leonards now for 12 years.

I have been writing poetry on and off since my son was a baby, it is only in the last couple of years that I have tried to get any published.

I suffer with chronic cervical spondylosis and am in a lot of pain, so writing poetry is very therapeutic.

My family are very special to me, and a lot of my inspira-tion comes from them.

Here I lie in a hospital bed,
With sixteen pillows stuffed under my head
Tubes are going in here,
And coming out there,
God, do I look a mess?
Just look at my hair
There are people with adenoids and gallstones,
And some with their arms in a sling,
There are varicose veins and
All sorts of pains,
And a patient I know has
To sit on a ring!
They wake you up early for breakfast,
Then knock you out early at night,
The time in between is so boring,
If I were a bird, I'm sure I'd take flight.
Visiting hours seems to drag by,
Nobody knows what to say,
'Thanks for the grapes and the oranges'
'No, I don't want one now, but tomorrow I may.'
Here comes the lady with haemorrhoids,
I think I'll pretend I'm asleep,
It doesn't bring smiles, hearing all about piles
If she tells me once more, I will weep.
Still, I'm due to be let out tomorrow
I'll say 'Toodle, ooo' to each one,
Though I've moaned, and I've groaned,
and I've grimaced,
I am grateful for all that they've done.

Jill McClean

The Eagles Have Landed

They came in their thousands
the denim-clad fans,
of the soft-rock cult groups.
Most of them fifty-something!
No one felt out of place.
For they had come to pay homage
to the group, that for us had epitomised
the seventies.
'The Eagles had landed', at the
stadium, in the centre of Huddersfield
And we were all ready to roll back
the years. It was not just for the
oldsters, there were many who had
come from miles around.
To this splendid stadium who had
heard, this band's music, in their
cots, from the first moment these
'ageing Americans' stepped on the
stage. They showed the crowds just
why their appeal is so enduring.
They started with their 'biggest hit'
and carried on from 'strength' to
'strength', playing to their converted
fans. 'Good Time Rocking'
'The Eagles had indeed landed.'
What a thrill indeed for young and old alike!

Sarah Ainsworth

The Mouse

Notes

Clive Mandry, aged forty seven, is married to Marian (his inspiration!). They have a daughter, Amanda, who is a college lecturer, and a son, Kevin, an electrician. Their cat, Topsy, has inspired him to pen a poem called simply *My Cat*.

He is a building contractor and runs his own business, he has only put pen to paper in the last twelve months.

His publications include: *Despair* in Sweet and Innocent, 1996, and *The Interview* in A Lasting Calm, 1997.

I may only be two inches high,
But prince am I of all I survey,
I live behind the skirting wall,
King and lord, 'the Belle' of the ball.

With pride my kingdom I survey,
My domain, dominion's high.
I swagger, I sway, a lion would roar,
But gigantic things I find such a bore.

I recently made the acquaintance
With the ladies of the house
They'd scream, they'd shout, they hollered,
'A mouse, a mouse, *a mouse*!

My cousin farmer field mouse
Came to visit for a while.
He brought a supply of kernels,
Oh did we dine in style.

The family is growing
'Space is tight' says Mrs Mouse,
It really is no problem,
We'll move to a larger house!

C L Mandry

Soul Mate

Notes

I am married with a grown up son and daughter and four grandchildren.

I started writing verse just last year mainly to pass the time. I have had three poems published in The Northern Echo; our regional newspaper, which runs a column featuring 'The Monday Poem'.

With your furry coat and saucer-like eyes
You captured my heart which was no surprise,
As you scampered around it was plain to see
You'd soon become part of the family.
I feed you and groom you and keep you clean
A smarter cat will rarely be seen.
My care and attention are not in vain -
You share in my pleasure and in my pain:
One day when my heart was sore
You touched my cheek with one soft paw;
You comforted me through lonely nights
And snuggled up purring, till things were right.
You seem to sense when I'm feeling low
With headache or backache or heartache and so
I tell you my troubles - you never complain
When I'm feeling down and start moaning again!

Audrey Raine

Notes

I began writing poems in 1992. Inspiration can strike at any time. I am 77 years old and live with my wife Bronwen in the village of Abercynon, South Wales. We celebrate our Ruby wedding in March.

Many of my poems have been published in my local paper. The majority of my poems refer to true life characters and events. I possess a terrific sense of humour which shows up in my poems. Two of the presenters on Radio Wales, Roy Noble and Frank Hennessy have included my poems in their programmes.

My interests are my family's achievements, pride in my grandchildren and great-grandchildren and the happiness we share together.

I dedicate this poem to a loving family!

Happiness

Happiness to me is life itself
Photos of my family, up there on the shelf.
In summer I enjoy the balmy breeze
The singing of the birds in the trees!

I love to stroll beside the sea
I certainly enjoy a cup of tea.
I enjoy living in my flat
Meeting people and having a chat.

I like having my grandchildren around
My weighing scale telling me, I've lost a pound.
I love to smell the grass being mown
But I'd never want to live alone.

Most of all I'm thankful I can see
Everything that goes on around me.
Good health is far more precious than gold
I'm not too happy about being old!

Norman Desmond Humphreys

Notes

Hi! I'm Marie, I'm 27 years old and live in a small village called Thornley in the County of Durham with my two daughters, Katie who is seven, and Amy, who is five. Both of them are very mischievous as you can imagine by the words of this poem.

But Mam, It Wasn't Me is dedicated to both my daughters Katie and Amy whom I love very much.

But Mam, It Wasn't Me

Mam, she got your make-up
Hurry and see
Cherry red all over her face
But Mam, it wasn't me.

Mam you know the washing
The ones that's nice and clean
They're lying up the garden path
But none of them have seen.

Mam she's in the bathroom
She's pouring out shampoo
I ran to try and rescue it -
Too late it's down the loo.

Mam you know the wallpaper
The one that you've just done
She's taken up a pen up there
She's having lots of fun.

Mam you know the flour
That you left over there
I think you'd better come and see
'Cause now it's everywhere.

Mam you'd better hurry
I dread what it might be
The answer to my question is
But Mam it wasn't me.

Marie Hedley

Notes

Many of my poems are written for people close to me and relate to circumstances, some good times and some bad times.

This poem was given to a friend who lost her husband under tragic circumstances in March 1996.

Therefore, I dedicate this poem to Allison.

Emptiness

I can't focus on the world anymore
I want it all to go away
Time seems to be standing still for me
Can't get by each passing day

A dark cloud is hanging above me
I'm feeling tired and so alone
Don't want to cry another tear
Or face this on my own

I'm putting on my brave face
Even though inside my body is aching
Can't think about the future anymore
As right now my heart is breaking

I wish the sun would shine for me
And brighten up my sky
As it's hard for me to smile today
No matter how hard I try

Wendi Harrison

Thru a Child's Eyes

Notes

Harry Michael Fox was born in Keighley, Yorkshire, right on top of the moors.

He has had some poems published in the Manchester Guardian when he was aged 10 and 11. When he was 15 he went into racing and became an apprentice jockey. He had a few rides for the Queen then got too heavy. At this stage he eased off his poetry writing, but began again in about 1960, although he kept throwing it away when it piled up.

In 1990 he had to take early retirement because of arthritis in both knees and hips so now he writes poetry as much as possible.

When I was two thru a misty hue
A fairy came to me all dressed in blue
Even right up to when I reached three
She always came and attended me
And when I was an unruly four
She played with me on the floor
I was convinced when I was five
My fairy to me was the only one alive
Gettin' brainy I reached seven
I knew my fairy came from heaven
Only one year did she come late
The year was me reaching eight
At nine I began to know what I'd got
My fairy, my own fairy, was another
What luck for me it was my mother.

H Fox

For Amy

Notes

My name is Kirsty Jaynes, and I am currently studying for a degree at the University of Wolverhampton.

This particular poem was written in memory of Amy, whom I knew from college. She died suddenly on the day of her first 'A' level exam.

I hope that in some small way this poem will keep her memory alive.

How long will the candle keep burning,
Before destiny blows out the flame?
Nobody is immortal,
And we can't live life over again!

We continue to search for explanation:
An answer, some reason . . . a link.
Death creeps up from behind and hits you;
It brings you back down: makes you think!

The only certainty of life is its ending:
Disappearing never to re-appear.
You arrive then depart really quickly.
For a short time we live; blindly, here!

What for us is the next level:
Where do we go when we die?
Some lives are shorter than others.
The only question is why?

K Jaynes

The Good Listener

Notes

Hi, I'm Pam Kirkham, 48 years old, married to Jim for 28 years. We have 2 sons, Matthew 27, who is married to Lisa, and Adam 25, who is still at home. We have a brand new grandson, Harry, who is delightful. My own 'mid-life crisis' has happened recently. I was made redundant after 30+ years as a working girl. However, I've solved my problem by becoming a 'nanny granny' to Harry and letting Lisa get back to work.

This poem was written for my friend Lynn after a long and tearful phone call. I'm pleased to say that she's got her life together and even though she's going through a divorce, she seems to be coping very well.

I dedicate this verse to her.

'He's left me' she said, and the tears wouldn't stop,
A 'rock solid' marriage that now is a flop,
'The vows that we made - till death us do part'
'Now thirty years later he's broken my heart!'
I sat and I listened at the end of my phone.
They once were so happy - now she's alone,
I remembered their wedding, so long ago,
He'd been in the army, and was her first beau,
Who could predict an end such as this
As they sealed their promises with a kiss,
At fifty years old she's to start over again.
What ever went wrong? She's in so much pain,
Try to be strong is easy to say,
Put on a brave smile and live day to day,
Take up a hobby, what could she do?
Evening classes could be just right for you,
What qualifications do I have to advise,
'How can I pretend to be very wise,
You'll have to find new directions in life,
As your own person, not somebody's wife,'
'Build up your confidence and self esteem,
You're a new woman - not some old 'has been''
She said she felt better after talking to me,
Maybe I should start charging a fee,
Set up in business, be my own boss,
As the best ever listener you'll come across!

Pamela Kirkham

Notes

My name is Mary Bernadette Evans and I was born in Birmingham in 1950. My father Bert died in 1960 just before my 10th birthday and my mother Eileen struggled to bring up myself and my three brothers. She died in 1987. I had an ordinary secondary modern education from which I gained four CSE's.

I married my husband Kenneth in 1970 and we had four children, Julie in 1971, Connie in 1973, Justin in 1974 and Natalie Jayne Louise in 1981. Natalie died from Leukaemia in 1995 aged just 13 years. She was a very special and beautiful child.

It was after Natalie's death that I started to write poetry and all my poems are dedicated to her. This poem will be the sixth one to be accepted for publication. One day I hope to write a book about Natalie's life and the devastation of her death.

Since Natalie died my husband and myself have taken a great interest in life after death and have had a message from Natalie through a reputable medium. I am also studying hypnotherapy and hope to qualify as a hypnotherapist shortly.

Heaven

I can't wait to get to heaven
Just to see you smile
I can't wait to get to heaven
Just to sit awhile
I can't wait to get to heaven
Just to hold your hand
And try to understand
Why you couldn't stay
Why God took you away
From me too soon
I can't wait to get to heaven
To end my pain
To be with you again
My darling child

Mary B Evans

They Don't Understand

Notes

I am 37 years old, single and live with my 10 year old dog, a border collie cross called Becky. My father died when I was 18 years old but my mother lives just 5 minutes walk away which comes in handy when I need a dog sitter.

I have two brothers, one older and one younger, both are married with children.

I live in Trowbridge in Wiltshire and work as a financial control supervisor (bought ledger and wages) for the local brewery, Ushers of Trowbridge.

This is my second poem to be published. My inspiration comes from everyday life, sometimes happy, sometimes sad.

They don't understand, all those well-meaning friends,
Of the need that she has that won't go away
For the things that they have but don't really see
A friend, a lover, a child, a life
A longing, so deep it cuts like a knife
A wound that runs deeper with each passing day
Her existence the nightmare that won't go away.

Sue Barnett

Notes

I was born and raised in London, but moved to Milton
Keynes in 1981, where there
are still plenty of fields and
open places left at the moment! I have submitted two
other poems, Apart From
Nature's Beauty Our Greed
and My Life is in a Turmoil
which have both been pub-
lished. I am chuffed, three
out of three poems, I hope
that they are enjoyed.

I am 49, married with four
grown-up children, three
sons and one daughter. My
daughter and one son live in
Australia. Two of my sons are
married and I have three
grandchildren; Chloe is
seven, Luke is two and Jake is
one.
Until two years ago I worked
in a residential home caring
for the elderly. I was retired
due to disability following
three operations on the spine.

I started writing poems when
my granddaughter was born,
the love and joy she bought
to my life inspired me to
write my first real poem. I
had written odes, but nothing
with meaning. I love to compose poetry about family,
people and life in general,
things that since becoming
disabled, have become important to me and my grandchildren's future.

Worn Out

There's lots of things in life you need,
And without care and attention will fail.
To learn how they work the instructions you read,
When they brake you fix them with hammer and nail.

But there's some thing's in life you just cannot mend,
So a new one you buy in its place.
To the tip the old ones you send,
Then soon the memories fade with no trace.

Clothes need washing and ironing,
The cooker needs cleaning too.
The car needs regular servicing,
And you cannot have a smelly loo.

Your clothes last longer with this care,
The cooker will last longer too.
Your car will always get you there,
The loo will be welcoming too

So how do you care and look after me,
You cannot mend me with a nail.
My worn out parts you cannot see,
But they are there without a fail.

I've been taken for granted and worn out,
The warning signs ignored.
It wasn't done on purpose no doubt,
But my heart and mind have roared.

It's shouting hey look at me, I'm here,
Wife, mother not cook or maid.
I'm only noticed when I shed a tear,
Or when I shout and my nerves are frayed.

So what I'm saying to you all,
I cannot be fixed, dumped or sold.
I'm fed up, worn out, and ready to fall,
So I need more care I'm getting old.

So just look at what I do for you,
I clean, cook, wash and care.
There'd be dust and cobwebs through and through,
When the day arrives when I won't be there.

So look after me like you do the car,
The bike and the football boots.
Then I can go on being your Ma,
And I won't be pushing up grave yard roots.

Christine Brown

Notes

I am 26 years of age, born in Walthamstow, London in 1971 but at the age of 3 my family emigrated to Sydney, Australia, where I was brought up until I returned to England in 1990 at the age of 19.

I have many goals, aspirations/ambitions and my hobbies include travel (one of the main reasons I remain in England, closer and cheaper to travel to most places), bungee jumping, catapulting, hang-gliding, parachuting/ascending/sailing, jet-skiing, snowboarding. One of my main personal goals is to 'wingwalk'. All my adventure /high adrenaline hobbies I have done for charities including Cancer Research, Research for the Blind, Children in Need and Mental Health which is the field of work I do, I would love to make a career out of it. I work in community care as deputy care manager, helping to rehabilitate ex-patients from long stay wards in a psychiatric hospital and one day (soon, I hope) I would like to manage my own care home for the mentally ill or for people with a learning disability.

I have been writing poetry ever since I was about 6 years of age and I have also written a couple of short stories and lyrics for a song. I have never (until now) listened to people in regards to publishing any of my work so there have never been prizes or awards given.

My present circumstances that are important to me are my job/career, my newly purchased house, car and jet-ski and my girlfriend and her two lovely daughters.

I would like to dedicate this poem to my biggest fan, as well as critic, my mum!

Sadness

Do you want to tell me troubles,
Do you want to tell me strife.
Can I help you with your worries,
On no! You've lost your wife.

I can't give you advice or console you,
I can't help to heal your heart,
Nor can I look to the future.
Or tell you, why God made you part.

Do you want to tell the children,
Their mummy loved them, this I know.
Would they believe what I tell them
Or do they think she did just up and go.

Now my shoulder, you can cry upon,
But my tears will also come,
Because although she was your second wife
Oh dear God, she was also *my mum*.

Dean Michaels

Notes

My name is Mary Holder - pen name Yvette Redding, born in London in 1937 and married to David. We have one daughter, Veronica. I am a housewife and have obtained awards in English Literature and English Language.

I enjoy writing poems and short stories and a few poems have been published. I have only been writing for a few years.

I endeavour, through my observation, to reflect the emotions and frailties of human life in all my works. I write mostly poetry, for or about children, wildlife, fantasy, everyday life.

My hobbies are: reading, music, sewing, other creative work and of course my writing.

Holidays of Youth

My mind wanders back to those bright summer days
When we were young, on our holidays
Down in the country, to Devon we went
Oh! The games that we played then, the hours we spent
Fishing and swimming, running with glee
Through meadows so green, Peter, Mabel, and me.
Long, hot sunny days, with no sign of rain
How I wish dearly we could do it again.
The cottage was lovely, with flowers galore
In garden, scented roses around the front door.
Delphiniums, foxgloves, proud, so tall
Stood to attention by ivy-clad wall.
Sweet smell of the honeysuckle, framing archway
Which we all ran through, in our moments of play.
'Twas our grandparents cottage, I still remember
All the happy times, from July to September.
The fruit orchard was great, to play hide-and-seek.
From behind pink-blossomed trees we would sometimes peek
To see if the 'catcher' was anywhere near
If they would find us we would tremble with fear.
At the end of the garden, meandered a brook
Where we would catch tiddlers, with small line and hook
The water was perfect, pure, clear, and bright
Sparkled like glass, through the sunlight.
A wooden boat that we used, moored up on the bank
Gave hours of pleasure, we had Grandpa to thank
For letting us use it, the fun that we'd share
Playing pirates, finding treasure, with not a care.
When we got hungry, Peter, Mabel, and me
There was home-made honey, delicious for tea -
My mind wanders back to those bright summer days
When we were young, on our holidays.
Parents and grandparents, all passed away
Poor Peter went last year, Mabel this May.
So I am the only one left, from this family -
Me? - Oh! I'm jolly old Jack - now aged eighty three!

Yvette Redding

My Boy Ben

Notes

I am a forty four year old
housewife and a mum to five
children. I've been married to
Terry for twenty years and
we live in Chingford, London.

This is my eighth poem to be
published. I've had five poems published by Anchor
books. I only started to write
poetry two years ago, after
my dearest mum, Beryl Howard, died after a long illness,
and I write to ease my pain.
I'd like to dedicate 'Butterfly'
to my mum who, now free
from pain, can be the delicate
butterfly and live on for me.

My one hobby, beside poetry,
is Ben, my brindle grey-
hound, he's a giant but so
gentle. I gave him a home
just eight months ago, and
I'm very fond of him.

I have a number one fan in
my dad, Clifford Howard,
who is also very good with
words, I like to think I get my
talent from him.

I hear his soft breathing.
I see him give a twitch,
I see his ears give a flicker.
I see his nose does twitch,
I hear his soft growl,
I hear his soft bark,
I bet he's pacing round that track,
I bet he's dreaming, there, he's back,
A home for Ben, he's found,
A big old brindle, greyhound,
So soft and gentle, yet so big,
He's really such a soppy,
And when he's really happy,
A lick you'll get, all sloppy,
He's very much a gentle soul, truly so serene,
He's still a truly magnificent sight,
So cute, so shiny, so clean,
And he loves me so very much,
This I can tell, by the wagging tail,
And his paw, so gentle to the touch.

D Campbell

Notes

I was born 26th March 1933 in Manchester. I was educated in a Secondary Modern School and obtained several GCEs. I have two children, a son and a daughter, and one granddaughter. My hobbies are gardening and writing.

I have had three poems published and have an award from The International Poems Association. I have written a novel, a short story and numerous poems.

My aim is to try to reach people through my poems, to write of my life and experiences which people can relate to their own.

Life

Life is just a journey along which each of us must travel,
Each day a different road or way, a lesson to unravel,
Each and every person we encounter on our way
Will teach us something different to either learn or say,
Each person is a wise-man or just a simple fool
And only we can understand to make or break each rule,
The journey takes us on our way, each step we take is fated,
Woven by life's tapestry of loves and hopes abated,
If only we could have the gift to see our future clear,
Would we find the heart to walk ahead, showing no more fear,
To climb the hills of sadness or the valleys of remorse,
To fight each battle as they come or fail at every course,
Only God can know our strength, our weakness or our fears,
And only we can walk our road, our journey through the years.

Violet Ashton Reid

Mum

Notes

I am 26 years old, I have two beautiful daughters, Lois Ann and Josie Marguerite, and I am married to Peter.

I have had ten of my poems published in various books. My greatest achievement was having the poems I wrote about each of my daughters published.

My inspirations come to me in many different ways - from simply walking down a road or from my dreams and most of all from my life. I eventually hope to publish my own anthology.

Washing, ironing, cook the tea,
Part of a busy day for me,
Changing nappies, wiping hands,
Naughty children ruined my plans.
No time now to go up the shop,
How I wish that clock would stop,
Hoover out, for a quick clean round,
Children asleep there's now no sound,
Alarm clock rings it's time to rise,
Get out of bed rubbing my eyes,
Chilly old morning, get slippers out,
Walk to the bathroom, the little ones shout,
Into their bedroom to get them dressed,
It's Sunday girls so let's wear our best.

D L Fryers

Notes

I am 34 years old and have been married to Irene for nine years. I have three children, Daniel 6, Kayleigh 2 and Ross 9 months. I live in South Queensferry just outside Edinburgh and am employed by the Ministry of Defence as a dog handler.

I am currently having three other poems published by The International Library of Poetry.

Given my occupation I am obviously interested in dogs particularly the German Shepherd variety. I also have a keen interest in cartoons, gardening and DIY.

On recalling an incident from my childhood when I fell into a river and was pulled out by my elder brother, I decided to put the experience into words in the form of a poem called *My Brother*. It is events like this, from my childhood to the present, which inspire me to write.

The poem opposite recalls an experience I'll never forget, I was nine years old and had been ill with severe stomach pains for a couple of days. Unknown to myself and my parents I had suffered a ruptured appendix which required emergency surgery. Only in later life after reading about near death experiences did I realise that what I thought was a dream, was in fact, such an experience, I think!

We live and learn.

It's Not Time

I wasn't well the pain was bad
I was only a young boy, a slip of lad
I lay in bed frightened and scared
When will the pain go will I be spared

Out of my bed I rose like a dove
Looking down on myself asleep from above
I'm strong and I'm young it's not time to go
Back into my body like an angel I flow

Flashing blue lights at speed I am taken
My pain was away as I stirred to awaken
There's always a good side to things as a rule
The good side in my case was six weeks off school

Colin Henderson

Zero

When I grew old
I tried a jar of vanishing cream
For wrinkles I had everywhere
This I didn't like, so they had to go
Then no more would show

It certainly worked well and fast
Now they are in the past
My face shone with a radiant glow
But my arms and legs looked an awful sight

I thought, why not do them as well?
Out came the jar I smoothed it on
A few months later all looked swell
But the mirror showed me even more

So delighted I applied even more
And found that worked just as well
It really made my skin shine
I felt absolutely divine

Then walking home one day
A sudden thought came into my head
Why not melt it down
And bathe in it instead

I hurried out purchased jars galore
And into the bath I did go
So inviting I couldn't wait to get in
So creamy, so white and so smooth

Oh how it felt upon my skin
When at last I climbed into bed
I felt like I had never done before
But much later when I opened my eyes

I got a real fright
My body nowhere in sight
I turned and saw an angel standing there
What happened I did say

He smiled and replied
Your body vanished, just clean away.

Prince Rhan of Kathari

Happy Childhood

I was once a little girl,
With my hair all in a curl.
Back then, I had a Mum and Dad,
But now heaven's got them,
(And I'm glad!)
Many happy years have swept away
Happy memories of the day
When Mum's dear lap, was cosy and warm
And Dad (God bless him)
Just looked on!
But now the years have quickly gone
Giving me the title 'Gran'.
All the off-spring (bless their hearts),
Do jolly well in taking part
To see that grans and grandpas too,
Reflect the lives
Of
Me and you.

Sylvia John

Love of King Cole

Notes

I've written a number of poems and they are all being published.

They are all on the theme of the homeless who sleep on the streets in the West End of London. I started the poem writing in January 1996 as, on my visits to the West End, I feel compassion for these people in distress. Also thoughts for the unemployed a start of a circle before the war. Relief tickets for food and beer, now it's a complete circle. Giro cheques for what?

Love of bygone days - on the dole,
Everything was great.
Sun and sand - wind and rain,
Jellied eels - bucket and spade,
All good things end,
A few years of black clouds.
Good years are promised again
Believe in me, said the man
I believed? I believe!
It's now, cut, cut, cut,
Nothing lasts forever,
But the sun will shine again,
Tomorrow is Giro day,
On the King Cole again.

Just Mac

Notes

I am the mother of 4 children and have 12 grandchildren. I love children and have looked after them all my life.

I write about anything, and about everyday life, I have written two poems for Princess Di while she has been so distressed, she wrote back to thank me for the comfort I gave her and told me to 'keep going',

The poem *Child's Thoughts* is about a little girl of 8 who, at Christmas time, was left alone while her parents drank. I asked her what was in her mind.

Football

I'm learning to play football
To be a footballer like my dad
To know the rules and kick a ball
Right into goal just like my dad
Crowds come to see me
And expect a lot from me
Just because I kick a ball
It's the hardest thing for me

L Rowland

The Hurting and the Heartache

Notes

To the special years.

The hurting and the heartache.
Always there with me.
You said 'Good morning my dear.'

The simple things you did.
The simple things you said.
Bring back those special memories of you.

Thank you for all the loving.
The caring and understanding
You showed me throughout the years.

Laughter and crying times
Are always best remembered.
Those special memories I will always keep of you.
Now it's time to say 'Goodnight my dear'

Sandra Hewlett

Notes

I am 41 years old, married with three children and I live in Lincoln.

I have many hobbies including swimming, gardening and animals and my main ambition is to drive a steam train.

I love writing poems and I have written about all aspects of life, this one particular poem I can relate to very well as I've had arthritis for ten years.

I dedicate this poem to all sufferers everywhere.

Arthur-itis

I don't like to say it
But it seems Arthur's struck again
For nearly every morning
He attacks me with this pain
Not that I've upset him
Or hurt him in any way
It's just that it seems to be the norm
For him to start the day
It started with the stiffness
Then the joints began to swell
And when you first try to get out of bed
Well it feels like you're in hell
You go to pick up your tea cup
And find that your fingers don't meet
And trying to open a cereal packet
Well that is no mean feat
And when you eventually get going
Your feet feel full of stones
Even though you're taking the tablets
Doesn't stop the aching in your bones
I've tried taking cod liver oil
And certain foods I'll avoid
But nothing seems to cramp the style
Of good old Rheumatoid
Sometimes he will fool you
And you'll wake up free of pain
Go and start weeding the garden
But then he comes back again
Steroid injections hold no fear
For Arthur and his army
Gold injections, Plaquenel
It's enough to send you barmy
I'll have to have some brand new hips
As my joints are crumbling fast
And in the meantime I'll just smile
Until our Arthur has past
But so what if your joints go all knobbly
And some days you can't get out of bed
Things could be a whole lot worse
After all you're not yet dead

J M Midgley

Secret

Notes

Janette Harazny née Melvin was born 1959 at Stockton Heath near Warrington, Cheshire. She has seven sisters and six brothers. She married in 1979 and she and Stefan have two daughters, aged 17 and 11. She was educated at Appleton Grammar School.

A semi-finalist in three recent competitions held by The International Society of Poets, she is receiving a certificate for outstanding achievement to poetry, aka the Editor's Award.

Poems published to date number twenty included in the anthologies: Voices on the Wind, Awaken to a Dream, Cream of the North West, Voices of the People, and Young at Heart, most of which were published by Anchor Books.

She has been employed at Tesco, Northwich for eight years and has written several poems for store staff. Beginning with competition slogans, she started writing seriously eighteen months ago.

A really unusual pastime
Says everyone who hears
What you and your man have indulged in
For many, many years
Taken you around the world
Maintained your fitness taboot
Your little secret becomes unfurled
And you don't give a hoot
The suspense is killing everyone
What is it that you do?
You both have the time of your life
On a bicycle made for two.

Janette Harazny

House of Memories

Notes

Deanne Jones is a middle aged housewife who has had some poems and limericks published.

She enjoys reading non-fiction and writing, and has had one children's story published.

Nature inspires her, as does good music.

Life has scratched vast memories
Across the once busy home
Fleeting shadows of souls departed
Through hall and attic roam

Fingerprints of days long gone
Lie there for you to find
All you need is imagination
A searching active mind

To look beyond cold empty rooms
Stark bare bone brick and damp
To behold in your mind's eye
Children reading by the old oil lamp

Inhale the dank sweet musty smell
Remember how things used to be
Let the voices of the past
Fill your heart with ecstasy.
          Ecstasy.

Deanne Jones

Lying in Bed

Notes

This poem is dedicated to my girlfriend, Kerry, who has always been there for me.

I can't sleep, I'm wide awake,
I'm waiting for the day to break,
the birds will sing, the cars will start,
a couple may just break apart.

I'm ready for what the day might bring,
so I'll sit and wait for the birds to sing.

I'll miss today it's been quite fun,
but bring me around another one,
one that's cold, wet or hot,
anything of what you've got.

So in the day will surely creep,
I'd say hello, but I'm fast asleep.

Asa Hillsey

Fond Memories

Notes

My name is Lynne, I am 33 years old, married with two children and live in Scunthorpe.

I first found an interest in poetry while I was at junior school. I have to say that writing poetry gives me great pleasure. Most of the poems I have written are about my family and friends.

I have had seven poems published in books and three printed in the local evening paper. I like to think that people get as much pleasure from reading my poems as I do in reading other people's work.

I never really told you how much I loved you so,
I loved you more than anyone could ever really show,
I kept my thoughts hidden deep inside,
My true love for you I could never hide,
My eyes held the secret that only I knew,
The secret of love I had only for you,
Deep in my mind love memories I kept locked away,
Memories to re-live together on our chosen day,
Far sooner than planned God took you for His own,
Now I'm the one with memories left here all alone,
Forgive me when I say 'Please don't be the one to cry'
I'm the one left alone with our memories I'll never allow to die.

L D Storey

Notes

My age is 77, I am a war veteran. I have a wife and married daughter, and two teenage granddaughters. I live in Dagenham, Essex

I am retired now, but I was a stationmaster on London Underground.

I have had two other poems published by The National Library of Poetry , namely *Night Reverie* and *Spring is Here.*

My hobbies are reading, writing poems, crossword puzzles, football and other sports (watching now).

I started writing short verses for my wife's birthdays and our wedding anniversaries, I started to do this about twenty years ago but since retiring have found more time to think of longer poems.

My inspiration for writing is the things in the world that happen to most people. I just pick on certain subjects and it goes on from that.

Nature

Nature is a wonderful thing
It has four seasons
The first is spring
This is the time new life is born
And heralds the beginning
Of a brand new dawn
Summer comes next
And with it we see
Glorious weather and scenery
The sun is stronger
The nights are longer
And holiday time is here
We welcome the freedom
From trouble and strife
And put back a springier step
In our life
But autumn upon us
Too quickly we fear
The nights will get shorter
At the end of the year
But we have good reason
To welcome it in
For the beauty we see
All around this season
Is a joy to behold
With the leaves in the trees
Turning glorious gold
But then we have winter
It's not very nice
It usually brings us
Much snowing and ice
It's so very cold
And quite bad for the old
But this is what nature
Is mostly about
That having four seasons
Will leave us no doubt
That we cannot have some
And leave others out.

W J Sermaine

Notes

Paul Snaith is 27 years old and lives in Darlington.

This is the second of his poems that Poetry Today have published.

Tonight We'll Begin, was the first poem he ever wrote and is about breaking through from unhappiness and realising that there is harmony on earth.

His inspiration for this poem was meeting a group of people who showed him a lot of happiness and so is dedicated to Elim Pentecostal Church in Darlington.

He is not a big church goer, but has found contentment and peace there.

His hobbies include playing the drums and he has recently recorded a CD which is on the market now. He also shows Welsh mountain ponies at the spring and summer shows.

Tonight We'll Begin

When I saw the dear old eyes,
The old lady smiled and looked surprised,
the way she looked at me tonight,
read to me that they were right,
Where before I was sitting with folded arms,
I am now awake and feel his charms
Where before I stood with my eyes shut
I feel my shackles now have been cut
Tonight I can sing like never before
My heart is warm and I want some more
tonight I think that all I see
Is how we all works so perfectly
We were moulded so identically
Yet set out on our own destiny
Not to explore our talents on this road
Would be not to water the seeds he sowed,
For ahead of us all is an exciting time,
I've even got this line to rhyme,
Tonight this here reflects on my mind
the warmth and harmony of mankind
all of us playing an identical tune
we pray that we'll return quite soon
In life it's important that we learn
We'll learn a little more when we next return.

Paul Snaith

Traffic

Notes

Traffic is my fourth poem to be published. Environmental issues are high in my priorities, and as I am soon to be a grandmother, it is even more important that we take care of our environment for the sake of our future descendant's health.

Ambition was my first attempt, since then I have written many more and will continue to do so. I find it very rewarding and therapeutic to write down your memories and inner feelings. This is true especially for the older generation, who I would encourage to try it.

So with hope for future health and happiness I dedicate Traffic to our future descendants.

Traffic speeding, up and down,
Picking up, and putting down
some for pleasure, some for gain,
A contribution, to acid rain.

In the cities, out of town
With soot and dust, that would astound
Wheel's grinding in the dust,
Of earth's very precious crust.

We must listen to advice,
Or our children will pay the price.

Evelyn Poppy Sawyer

Notes

I scribble for my own enjoyment, as I am 82 years old
and a pensioner. My husband
is terminally ill, which means
I cannot get out much. So I sit
and think up poems, and put
them in an exercise book.

I did write one poem, for a
relative, who was coxswain
of Padstow Lifeboat for many
years, he was Trevor England
OBE. He had the poem
printed in the local newspaper.

A couple of years ago I wrote
a book about 'life, events,
people, sayings and the ways
of entertainment' from before
1900 and through my life-
time. I have all the postcard
pictures of events covering
100 years to go with the
book.

Unobservant

I thought a walk I would take
Across the moors, to see the lake,
As I tramped along, the views to see,
Beautiful heathers, filled with
Birds and bees,
Then I had the urge to have a wee,
But as I crouched,
Alas! I did not see
That nettle. Oh! how it stung me.

Doris Richards

Notes

I was born in the North of India, not far from Kashmir, it is called Meerut. My mother was also born there, but in Kashmir itself. I was born on 15 November 1928. I have travelled a lot all over India, from the time I was a babe. When I was 18 months, we all left for 'Blighty', we returned in later years after my Pa died.

I was schooled at boarding schools in Agra, Allahabad and Bangalore. I was taught to sew, embroider, knit, cover books, type etc.

I am now retired and live in a nursing home.

I have two sons, and my daughter only lived for two hours. I saw some of my grandchildren in '84, the eldest was then 15. I have 7 grandchildren, two of them are in Germany, perhaps I'm a great-gran by now!

Since June 1996, I have had 15 poems published, four in semi-finals and one in a final, maybe I will be lucky.

My inspiration comes from God, the past, children, memories etc.

This particular poem is dedicated specifically to Jenny, my hairdresser, she's tops.

The Hairdresser

I've found another friend
Since I came here to live
Once a fortnight, she does come
She comes to visit me
A visitor I call her
That really isn't true
She's Jenny my hairdresser
Who stops me feeling blue
She is so friendly to us all
She listens to my tales
It's really fun to visit her
And get things off my chest
And when I walk away from her
I'm proud of what she's done
She really is a good friend
To me and everyone.

S Wall

Notes

I am 86 years young, with a loving family of five children, 14 grandchildren and 15 great-grandchildren: more than half of these are living in Australia. My wife and I have visited them several times.

We have a 'Family Poetry Book' in which most of our family and some friends have contributed their thoughts and feelings in verse.

I served 15 years in the Royal Tank Corps which included war service, 1939-1945, and was awarded five campaign medals.

I have been writing poems for pleasure since I retired. None published.

The *Trees* which I submitted to you, was inspired by the Year of the Trees.

I am interested in natural history, I love gardening and enjoy walks in quiet country places with a dog by my side.

Invitation to a Ramble

Come and take a ramble with me
You who were born to be free
Free to face the wind and rain
Free to wander over the plain
There are so many wonderful things to see
Created by God and all for free.
Listen; to the blackbird singing in yonder tree
Like an echo, then continue singing a song
The nightingale at dusk, to hear him is a must.
So let's ramble from daylight to dusk
We will take sandwiches and rest by the stream
The kingfisher flitters by.
With colours to match the rainbow in the sky
The water in the stream so clear
Makes the darting fish seem near
Does this not cause you delight
There is no sound that will cause you distress.
When down the country lane we wander
Away from the bustle of the human race
Out in the country is the place
To destroy beauty that's real.
Hurts like hell to one like me
Who hears music; from the wind in the tree,
Majestic they stand, for a century or more
History they have made in this pleasant land.
Has not the ramble been a surprise?
Even if you have been tormented by flies.
Like the bees they have a job to do
To pollinate the blossoms, which produces a scent so rare
God put a nose on our face
So such a smell is not lost in space
Don't envy me, get up and join me
For each day, you take a ramble
New interests you would gain, I'd gamble
Be alert, try your luck
I'll be your companion and your guide
And remain constant by your side

A C Marsh

Santa Claus

There's a man all in red
at the end of my bed
he's filling my sock to the brim
he has a big beard
that really looks weird
I think it could do with a trim
he has a red suit and big black boots
and a red hat on top of his head
and I don't care for the length of hair
it's making a mess of my bed,
but I better sleep or my presents he'll keep
and I'd be sad to say
I got up in the night and
gave him a fright and Santa
Claus ran away.

Linda Gibbs

Notes

I am 42 years old, and I have six children, three girls, three boys, ages 23 to 8 years. I have written poetry about them as they have grown up. I have one grandson who is a year old.

I live on Hayling Island, a holiday resort in Hampshire.

I write poetry on many subjects, this is my second to be published.

I am hoping to write a book of poems in the near future as I love poetry very much.

My poems come from many things. I hear a saying or see something and a poem begins in my head. My daughter Charlotte shares my love of poetry and has written some herself.

I would like to dedicate this poem to my family; my husband Trevor, my daughters Suzie, Jennifer and Charlotte, my sons Christian, Michael and Daniel and my grandson Joseph.

My dream is to have a book of my work published in the future so I have left something worthwhile behind me that others may enjoy.

Snowdrop

The snowdrop pops its tiny head
Above the snow so white,
It reaches for the sky above so
It can see the light.
It glistens like a shiny star
That everyone can see,
Or like a gemstone from afar
It shines for you and me.

June Clear

Memories

Memories can be full of sadness
or tinged with joy and gladness,
when you think you have forgotten
and the memory has faded away,
that's when you recall it
and realise it's here to stay

A memory is like a drop of rain,
here one moment and then gone again,
it can lift your spirits up to the sky,
or kick your dreams into try,
memories are precious and that is why
we all need them to survive.

Sylvia R Brace

I was born in May 1941 in Rochford, Essex. My growing up was accomplished between there and Kingston upon Thames. I met my husband in 1957 and we were married at St Mary's Church, Thames Ditton in June 1961. We had our first son while living in Surbiton and my daughter was born in Billericay, Essex and my two younger sons at Orsett. I was widowed in 1987 and now live with my five dogs and one cat, son and daughter-in-law.

I wrote my first poetry in 1957 but this is the first time I have submitted one for publication. All my writings have been prompted by a special time or event and some are very personal.

The last holiday I spent with my husband was on Jersey in 1986. It was a 25th wedding present from my mother and will always have great memories for me.

Jersey C I

This very beautiful island
With shores so rugged and wild,
Set my heartbeats racing,
Excited as a child.
Cliffs which shear so steeply,
Green fields which slumber deeply.
The soft brown eyes of the cattle
Contrast with relics of an ancient battle.
These things make a desire so deeply burning
To cause much haste in my returning.
To the island of so many dreams;
With sea-bed creeks dancing with sunbeams.
I've still many hills and cliffs to climb.
I will return ere too long a time.

Mollie Ridgers

Notes

I was married to my late husband for 33 years. I have been a widow for 3½ years and have three daughters, Yvonne, Dianne and Lindsay. I have lived in Lancaster all my life and love this city of ours.

I started off writing about our town and I have had quite a few poems printed.

I wrote the poem *Did You See?* for my friend Myra who was going to Australia on holiday last year.

I always liked poetry but did not start writing it until a year ago. Like your advert for poets, I saw one in our free paper and that is how I began. I will always be grateful to editor Andrew Head of Anchor Books who gave me my first chance.

My hobbies are: crosswords, reading, television, writing letters and books.

Did You See?

Did you see the famous
duck-billed platypus?
Did you see a kangaroo
hopping in the bush?
Did you see an emu
the bird that cannot fly?
I know if I'd been with you
they would have caught my eye

Did you see a wombat
sitting in the breeze?
Did you see koala bears
climbing in the trees?
Did you see a possum
or a dingo dog or two?
Bet your life you would have
if I had been with you.

Francine L

Notes

David Bowie once sang . . .
'We could be heroes, just for
one day . . .' The poem in this
book is in respect of some of
mine. For every songwriter,
composer, producer, musi-
cian or rock star whoever
worked on or recorded a
song that helped me focus my
vision in a life that can sometimes leave me feeling lost
and in need of some guid-
ance. In the words of John
Lennon, Sting, Bono and
Adam Ant respectively:
'Living is easy, with eyes
closed . . .' 'Be yourself, no
matter what they say . . .'
'Don't let the bastards grind
you down . . .' 'Ridicule is
nothing to be scared of . . .' I
rest my case.

What I Used to Be

I used to want to run where the streets have no name,
I used to want to flee on a runaway train,
I used to want to sail away on a ship called Dignity,
I used to want to fly like an eagle, that is free.

I used to want to hide away from the world outside,
I used to want to tame the animal deep inside,
I used to want to walk the long and winding road,
And cast from my shoulders all life's heavy loads.

I used to hope the sun would never go down on me,
As an island, or a rock is a lonely thing to be,
Whenever there was trouble I had to let it be,
The fool on the hill, the nowhere man, that's what I used to be.

Sometimes I used to feel as though I must break free,
Like a caged up lion, set free the beast in me,
I used to long for love to come and rescue me,
I thought if I turned a different corner,
This existence might not be.

I used to spend my life always running scared,
Whenever problems came my way I never was prepared,
I used to live up to someone's image of myself,
Who wants to be a dusty book left sitting on a shelf.

All these things I used to be have helped to make me strong,
I've learned from past experiences as my life has moved along,
I've given up on sorrow and I've given up on pain,
Things no longer bother me, I've learned to live again.

C Sanwell

Notes

I am 41 years of age, married with three children. I served in the army for five years and have worked in the building trade for twenty years as a felt roofer. I was born in a place called Etruria in the heart of 'the potteries' but now reside in Little Dimsdale, Newcastle-Under-Lyme.

I started to write short comical verses about nine years ago mainly for the amusement of my wife. I never really kept any of the earlier poems I had written, I used to write them and throw them in the bin.

I cannot actually say what inspires me to write, it is not other poetry because I've never read any, also I never plan to write, it's either there or it isn't.

I wrote this poem to celebrate the birth of my daughter, Samantha Victoria, whom I love very dearly.

A Father's Love

The day you came into my life
Emotions that I felt
Your tiny hands and feet
You made my heart melt

I held you in my arms
And knew that this was love
My head was in a whirl
And I thanked God above

A gift from your mum
A celebration from on high
The produce of our love
Will last until I die

A love so beautiful
In every way
What more can a father give
Do, feel or say.

S E Moult

Notes

I am Maureen Beatrice Arnold born 19 July 1939 in Edmonton, North London. My parents are Mrs, and the late Mr Alfred Philip Goodrich, both from Tottenham, North London. I have been happily married to Brian Samuel Arnold for 37 years. We have two children, Tracy and Ryan.

Tracy and her husband Gary have given us three beautiful grandchildren and they, of course, are *The Three Degrees* in the poem. Ryan and his fiancee Vicky are getting married in July this year.

I work as an ancillary worker at our local doctors' surgery. Apart from writing poetry, my hobbies include; reading, gardening, cooking, holidays abroad, walking the dog and spending as much quality time with my grandchildren as I can.

I first sent work to be published at Brian's suggestion in 1996 and have been delighted at the results. Apart from *The Three Degrees*, I have had work published by yourself in your beautiful book *Mists of Time*, also Forward Press, Bookmark Publications and the International Library of Poets.

I also write poetry for our British Legion's own quarterly magazine.

The Three Degrees

I peeped into the bedroom, to see if he was alright.
'I haven't been able to sleep yet Nan, as I forgot to say night night.'
Goodnight, God bless you little one,
You are growing up so fast you know, my 12 year old grandson.

I open the door to the spare room, to check that the other two are asleep.
I kiss them gently on the cheek, and to the door I slowly start to creep.
'We are awake, Nan' two voices cry, 'We fooled you that time for a while,'
'You certainly did you rascals,' I say, trying to hide a smile.

Wasn't it only yesterday, my own children were as small
as the three of you,
Small, trusting and vulnerable, blonde hair and eyes so beautifully blue.
It certainly seems like yesterday, so I must make these memories last.
And all I would ask of you little ones is please don't grow up too fast.

Maureen Arnold

Mum and Dad

I stand alone in a garden
A garden of peace and rest
And I think of my Mother and Father
Who were truly two of the best

We were poor but happy in childhood
It was they that made it so
It broke our hearts to say goodbye
When the time came for them to go

But if there is a heaven up yonder
Then we must truly feel quite glad
That by God's side sit two loving people
I mean my lovely Mum and Dad.

D M Herring

A Pet For Life (With RSPCA in Mind)

Notes

Barbara has had many poems published. Her main aim is to open a craft shop for disabled people. As she is partly deaf herself, she appreciates that being disabled is viewed as a stigma. Barbara feels that by giving the disabled a chance in a craft shop they gain their independence. She feels that it may only be a dream as she cannot raise the funds to get it going.

We may look cute and cuddly,
Especially when we're small,
But please don't give us at Christmas time,
As we're not always loved by all.

Please don't hit us, we don't understand,
The meaning behind the savage hand,
We have to learn all about your rules,
Especially if we make a few pools.

We learn by simply being told off,
For puddles on the floor,
But really, it's not much fun for us,
If we're cast out, and you shut the door.

Please consider just what's involved,
Before you decide to buy,
We all value your love and your friendship,
And with this in mind, we will then try.

Try not to chew your slippers,
Or climb to your curtain rails,
All it needs is that word called 'No,'
Believe you me, it never fails.

If you treat us with your kindness,
We will repay you, with our love,
But please don't cast us out because we're small,
As it's really not much fun at all.

All I can say is, 'You've helped ease the pain,'
Because I belong to a family again,
But I'm still wondering what I did so wrong,
In the home before this, where I didn't belong.

Barbara Holme

My Garden

My garden is like a church
The body to rest, the mind to search.
All the wonders of this magic place
Makes life's problems easier to face.

There's no place like it anywhere
Just relax, and sit, and stare
At the beautiful colours all around
Pure nature, hardly a sound.

Just the birds, and the busy bees
Flying about as they please,
The wind gently blowing through the trees,
Thank God for that lovely breeze.

John Atkinson

The Thrush

Notes

I wrote this poem after watching a beautiful thrush build her nest twice in my garden. I like to think she brought her family to my garden to show me she had at last been successful. God had indeed answered my prayers.

I watched you build your first nest
in the old fir tree.
Gathering straw and moss and mud,
how cosy it would be!
Until a magpie came to call and
smashed your eggs all three.

I watched you build your second nest,
in the laurel hedge.
You were sitting happily upon your
eggs.
Until the strong north wind blew
and tore it all to shreds.

I didn't see you for a while.
Though, I looked for you each day
when you called this afternoon.
I really had to smile.
I knew God had answered my
prayer.
When I saw you, so proud, with your
family standing there.

Angie Clark

The Voice of Amanda

Notes

I am known as 'The Fossil' by friends and natives around here. I am 68 going on 18, yes I am antiquated. I have recently written about my life as a child in the thirties for a local school. It must have interested them as I was asked to write more which I have done. I did not realise I could remember so much, I am history, living history.

I still bike ride every day, weather permitting, which I have done all my life. I come from a family of athletes, my father was a shot putter and hammer thrower and mother was a county hockey player. Cycle training becomes a lifetime habit, like cleaning your teeth. I do not boast, but I am able to endure physical strain more than people half my age in this area. Cyclists like myself are regarded as crazy, let me assure you, we are!

Amanda Thompson
Was born with an extra lung,
In church on Sunday,
When hymns are sung,
You can hear her voice
All over town,
Even God himself,
Has to turn the sound down.
Her powerful voice drowns out
The noise of cars,
Her voice was heard
In the vicinity of Mars,
Because her voice
Can be heard in space,
She speaks on behalf
Of the whole human race.

D G Field

Old Age

Notes

I was born in a small Cornish village called Tywardreath, where I also went to school. From the time I could read and write I have loved *words* and usually came top of my class with compositions and English work. Many of my poems have been read to patients in hospitals and hospices and I'm told they have given great comfort.

I love to write both poetry and stories; my *unwinding* comes from varied dancing and I'm a member of The St Austell Follies. For *anyone* to read my efforts and enjoy them is a great pleasure and honour to me and I feel pride at being one of the lucky ones chosen to take a part in Poetry Today for the second time. My first poem being *In Memory of You* in the Rhyme and Reason edition. Achievement is an aid to survival!

I'm old and I'm wrinkled I sit in my chair,
Eyes dim and faded, but memories are there
Of family and children, of lovers and life,
Of sorrow and glad times, of pity and strife.
My heart beats much slower
I look for the night,
My hands gnarled, are shrunken,
My eyes squint at light.
Old age has crept on me, my beauty has gone
Forever behind me as death comes along,
My youth smooth and shining is set to decay,
My hair long and golden, now dull, thin and grey.
But I have such stories of love in my head
To cherish, remember until I am dead.
My life has been torment
I've known deep despair
I've lived on light laughter, and grief has been there.
I've known all these feelings
I've *lived*, so I'm told,
To laugh, to *remember* them
Now that I'm *old!*

Margaret Hanning

My Love For You

Notes

I am 34 years of age. I am married with three boys, Nick 13, Martin 11 and Dale 9. My husband is Mark and I live in New Milton, Hampshire.

I enjoy working with children as I am a special needs assistant at New Milton Junior School.

I have been writing poems since I was young.

I get my inspiration from children, having a younger brother and sisters, also children of my own and working with children.

My love for you is strong and deep,
It makes it so I cannot sleep.
My love for you just grows and grows,
It keeps me always on my toes.
My love for you is day to day,
It helps me when I see you play.
My love for you is in the air,
It makes it so I'm always there.
My love for you is ever strong,
When I teach you right from wrong.
My love for you has just begun,
Because you are my beautiful son.

Dawn Croft

Destiny/Fate

Notes

I am Anthony Fidler, aged 41, married with two children, Matthew 3 and Katherine 16. Also a foster child, long term, called James, who is 6.

I am an assistant officer with Rochdale Social Services, I work with people who have a learning difficulty or handicap.

There are two other poems I have had published with The International Society of Poets; *This Bloody War* - Between a Laugh and a Tear and *My Chair* - Quiet Moments, both anthologies out this year, prizes still to be awarded.

Things special to me are working with disabilities, my wife and I also give respite to children with a handicap and we also have a foster child, our youngest has cerebral palsy, he is very special.

My hobbies are writing poetry, walking, climbing and making picture mirrors.

I started writing about 12 months ago. One night in bed I had a sentence in my head, that would not go away. I put it down on paper so I would not forget and finished up writing a seven verse poem.

I am inspired by people today, by the number of injustices that are done to others less fortunate than myself. People are frightened and do not take the time to understand people with disabilities, but are quick to condemn. I can put myself, I feel, in their place, and just to highlight their plight gives me great pleasure, my poetry is also very variable.

Two years ago my eldest brother died, and I needed to be alone, there is one place that he and I liked. At times I can take myself off and be alone at this place, at the top of Blackstone Edge near Littleborough, Lancashire. He is with me.

Destiny - fate, like the
Sands of time
They rule our heart
They rule our mind.

Just like the winter,
Spring and summer
Love is being there,
For one another.

The life we lead
We have but one,
Through a field of dreams
Until it's done.

Destiny, fate it's all
The same,
This life we have
Is just a game.

So when you find
The one you love,
It's fate that's shone,
From those above.

Destiny, fate like the
Sands of time,
Has sealed your heart,
With that of mine.

So now our days
Are nearly through,
Destiny calling, both
Me and you.

In heaven, we'll be together,
Like the sands of time
Forever and ever.

A Fidler

Notes

Divorced with a handicapped daughter. Have had a varied life, including some years in H M Forces, until the time I married, and had my daughter. No chance of any further career for the next 21 years, until my daughter went to an establishment suited to her needs.

Have devoted many years since to the care of the elderly and disabled. Now retired, and finding more time to write.

Started writing verses and won some children's prizes from Enid Blyton competitions. Inspiration comes easily, feelings, events, current affairs etc.

A poem in print, *Inspirations from East Midlands*, and a book (put together for my own enjoyment) accepted by International Society of Poets.

Father-in-law

My father-in-law was a wonderful chap
You never saw him without his cap
Winter or summer, rain or shine
He was in his garden, with a piece of twine
Tying, digging, cutting, pulling a weed
We'd say, 'Slow down' but he wouldn't heed
Then came the inevitable day
When his gardening tools were put away
He was ill, and lost, couldn't understand
Who would look after his piece of land.
He's gone away to a land of love
Rest in peace Alf, with the Lord above
On my list of friends you were at the top
I was proud to know you and call you Pop.

M Pearson

Notes

My name is Janet Elizabeth Heninghem and I live in Hertfordshire. I am a divorced mum of 45 and have been writing poems since I was a young woman. I write about all kinds of emotions and events that have happened in my life.

I have had one poem published by the International Society of Poets and have lots of other poems which reflect my feelings as an ordinary woman experiencing life as I see it.

If my poems reach the heart of the person reading them then I feel very honoured.

I feel blessed that I have three beautiful daughters and that God is looking down on me.

My First Divorced Christmas

Two days before Christmas and my mind goes back
To the Decembers of fun before disaster struck
The warmth and laughter all around
Now the family is broken
Santa's fell down

One tiny cracker laying by the side of
One straggly tree losing its pride
No children laughing and tearing the string
Just me and my memories, nostalgia can be a terrible thing
But I brought up three daughters who love me I know
Their Christmas will still be special
My heartache won't show

Because their father and me could not work ourselves out
Their Christmases are sadder without a doubt
Memories, memories, please keep you place
Let me get through this time, please for God's sake
But tonight I don't feel happy, I feel really sad
Remembering the happy Christmas times we once had
Before it all went bad.

Janet Heninghem

Channel Crossing

People huddled in muffled talk,
laugh too loudly, hold their drinks askew.

Children playing cards and Scrabble
giggle, nudge and push each other.

Young boys touch young girls' hair,
lips together, burning passion,
bodies posing, quite absurd.

Mothers hold their babies tightly,
wipe tear-stained cheeks and sticky hands.

The boat heaves gently, curtains sway,
The coast of Calais winks sublimely
England is a whole life away.

Penny Altmann

The Inquisitive Child

As the sun sets in the sky
I ask myself why?
Oh, why does it have to be so cold?
Why do we have to grow so old?
Why do I have to go to school?
Who one earth made such a rule?

My mother says don't worry son
Soon the morning will come
She just doesn't understand
That, that isn't so grand
As tomorrow I have to go to school
Why can't I stay home and act the fool?

Why do I have to learn such things?
Just see what tomorrow brings
Maths and French and history too
Why can't I just go to the zoo?
Why can't I do as I please?
Do I really have to pray on my knees?

Why are parents so unfair?
They just don't seem to care
I've all this information in my head
How on earth can I go to bed?
I guess I'll never know why?
So all I can do is sigh.

N Tucker

The American Roach

The dreaded cockroach hides everywhere,
Under the carpet and under the stairs,
Scuttles along rip, tip, tap, tap,
Under the chair and under the mat,
Runs like the clappers, full speed ahead,
Hides in the skirting and under the bed,
Ready to pounce when lights are all out,
Waits there in silence, but always about,
Crispy and crunchy, enormous in size,
Creepy and crawly, with devious eyes,
Dirty, disgusting an horrible sight,
Beware the American cockroach, especially at night!

Janice Walker

Notes

I am 38 years of age and my hobbies include: photography, art and interior design as well as writing.

Thank you to all my family and friends for all your support and encouragement, and a big thank you to Micky for encouraging me to submit my work.

Since having my first poem published in *Mind's Eye*, I have now reached my sixth. Three of these are in the semi-final competition for various anthologies.

I now live in Worksop, Nottinghamshire.

The American Roach is based on experience, having visited Orlando four times, I can honestly say, the roach is my worst nightmare. I would rather stand outside in a fully blown American thunderstorm, than come face to face with the dreaded roach!

Wireless Memories

Notes

I am a retired school teacher
and a member of the Uni-
versity of the Third Age,
North West London branch.

I belong to a poetry work-
shop there and my tutor is
Tamar Segal. Tamar is a
community poet.

Every week we went to town
For the accumulator
From Mr Brown.
If we forgot there'd be no play
To make a Saturday evening gay.
Wilfred Pickles, J B Priestley,
Tommy Handley, Henry Hall,
Dick Barton, Uncle Mac,
I loved them all.
To 'Housewives Choice' I'd sweep and dust
The 'Radio Doctor' was a must!
With 'Forces Favourites' I would sing.
Oh! How I crooned along with Bing!
Alvar Liddel reading the news,
The 'Brains Trust' airing their serious views.
These are the things that I remember,
These are my 'roses in December!'

Irene Igbinedion

Notes

My real name is Sylvia and I'm in my early sixties living in the small market town of Honiton.

Recently widowed, with three grown up daughters, (the eldest of whom lives in Australia), and four grandchildren in England. Before my marriage I was a professional actress and trained at L A M D A working in various repertory companies.

Have recently written a book called 'The Adventures of Elsie and Mabel,' being inspired by my daughter Amanda and hope it will be published soon. This poem is dedicated to the memory of my late husband Alec.

I like reading and classical music.

The love of poetry came at an early age while at boarding school and the years spent in the country as an evacuee; which gave me such pleasure in my surroundings. I am an only child but was never a lonely one, for I could find the time to stand and notice the things around me, always with a book and a pencil in my hand. I have not done any writing for many years but now find the time to do so therefore being able to give to my grandchildren the precious gift of the written word.

Growing Old

Old in years I may be, skin wrinkled like a prune,
But young at heart, that's me,
They say you can't dress mutton as lamb,
I don't care no way will I vegetate,
So out comes my flashy dresses hats and all,
Shoes that have a zing of colour,
Not black and sensible, that's not for me,
An OAP I may be, but life isn't going to pass me by,
No way,
Sitting at home alone drinking tea,
Eating seedy cake and watching TV,
That's not for me,
Oh no dancing and whizzing around,
In my little red beetle, that's me!
Shame on you my neighbours say, 'tut, tut,'
Be your age an OAP you are,
But when I die I'll go out with a *'bang,'*
That's me.

Alexis Peters

Notes

I am aged 53, married with one daughter and live in Nelson, Lancashire.

I write mainly for pleasure and some of my poems have been published.

I have been writing on and off for twenty-five years and started when I first met Pauline, my wife. Any kind of subject or phrase can trigger me to write.

The reason for this poem was how a simple choice can alter your life.

Philosophy of Life

Standing here without company alone
Feeling your heart turn to stone
For stone you can easily break
Your whole life can be changed by one mistake

You can lose all from what life you did gain
Fill your soul with nothing but pain
Life can teach us so very much
Even when It's soul we cannot touch

Life? Has meanings which can be so deep
From most of us its secrets it does keep
We always think that we understand
About any of life's plans that are so grand

But when we think what do we really know
Of how far it can take us if we should want to go
Its paths have many a twist and turn
Many of its moods we need to learn

Life can make you want it all
Take to a high, then set you up for a fall
Of your life, you must be in command
You have to rule it with a firm hand

Life's decisions must be full of thought
Or with many obstacles it will be fraught
As to your path, carefully make the choice
Listen to that quiet inner voice

For if you do not think it through
A sad and sorry life is in store for you
Make the choice, and life enjoy but not alone
And stop your heart turning to stone

Peter Howarth

The Camera

Notes

I am 62 years old, was born in St Albans and moved into the country village of Welham Green when I married Fred - just under 40 years ago. We have two wonderful sons, Andrew and Martin, who are both married and we have two very thoughtful daughters-in-law, Aileen and Debbie. As an added bonus I have three lovely grandchildren: Matthew, Jennifer and Robert, and a precious dog (Cairn Terrier) called Sandy.

I work part-time in the local pharmacy, Kean Chemist; I have been there almost 18 years and I meet a lot of interesting people.

My hobbies are: writing poems, reading, listening to music, and also painting. I also love gardening when the 'old bones' will allow. I'm very interested in wildlife: the stopping of cruelty to all kinds of creatures on this planet is very close to my heart.

I used to go to college and started to write very short stories just for my own pleasure. I started to write short poems in 1989 but never bothered to have them published until now.

It is circumstances which trigger me off writing, for example: people, places, just a moment's thought, happiness and sadness too.

I'd like to dedicate the poem to dad who is 93 years old and to mum who is 84 years old. Two wonderful parents.

Owning a camera can be fun
On holiday or just out in the sun
At Christmas time, the merry season
Snap the grandchildren, don't need a reason
Rush to the shop to get them printed
It was twenty four hour service, so I sprinted
Next day back to the shop to pick them up
Back home exhausted I made a cup
Of tea and took a look at my handiwork
Heads and feet cut off, what a jerk
I'm no David Bailey that's for sure
Next time I'll have to try a bit more

P Youngs

Too Pretty ~ Tom

Notes

I am 28 years old and live in East London with my cat, Sidney. My interests include: music, drama and all kinds of creative art.

I am currently doing voluntary gardening work within a project run by Newham Mind. I enjoyed many months meeting with a Newham Minds' poetry group, and had several poems printed in their first anthology, *To Grow a Row of Corn*, published in March 1994.

I have been writing poetry for as long as I can remember. I find it works as a kind of therapy, in the same way as others might choose to keep a diary. I write to somehow document, organise and express the thoughts and feelings that circulate in my mind. It is especially heartening to find that other people relate to these ideas.

I dedicate this poem to Margaret and Babushka.

Velvet nose flanked with whiskers of white,
'M' for Mohammed, he's just out of sight,
Black glossy stripes interspersed with grey
Two pairs of white socks, Persil clean every day,
Twitching tail, ever alert and so ready,
Luminous gaze, so compelling, so steady
Pencil sharp claws, scratching the floor
An excess of nipples, who can guess what they're for?
Super-fit body with an unfair share of grace
Slightly *too pretty* Tom with a beautiful face,
How empty it would be . . . here in this flat,
Without my ever faithful and most
Loyal friend . . .
                Sidney the cat.

S Shipley

Mr Typical

Notes

Born 17th March 1978, I have lived in the same house, with my mum, step-dad, twin sister and older sister, for eighteen years, in Barrow-in-Furness.

I started writing poetry and fiction from the young age of twelve, and have written five short stories, over fifty poems and am currently on my second novel, A World of Opportunities.

This year has been the best year of writing, for me. Due to unemployment I have had so much free time to produce work. By using such creative talent, I find it easier to put my feelings into words, and therefore, sometimes find writing as a therapy. Such poems displaying this have been *My Destination, Just Now, People, Your Way* and *Inside the Clouds.*

Six of my poems are to be published in separate anthologies, all by different companies..

Hobbies:- writing, television, films and music.

Your a Johnny
Of them men behind the curtain
A staggering, flickering flame
That boy of mine
He hasn't got a thing to shame

Walking down the path
Astride the shore are sea-shells
He grins mischievously
Knowing what he's got planned

Sparkling eyes
I only see them in my nightmares
You're a cushion for me
Sometimes you're my enemy

A shot at the best
So you follow the rest
Joining them in that love nest
But guess what?
You forgot me

T Charters

The Cottage

Notes

I am Amy Childs, nee Bow-
ditch, a widow, living in
Beaminster.

I lived at Toller Whelme for
several years, 1924-1926.
My father was carter on the
farm at that time and my
parents lived there again in
later life.

It stood in a field at the bottom of the farm
The bright summer sun keeping it warm
Roof of thatch, windows small
Just one door to enter by one and all

There was a living room and a scullery small,
That was alright if you weren't too tall,
The floor was just stone, the scullery just chalk
Mum put down rush mats on which to walk.

We had a large settle six foot tall
Cleverly place to form a hall
It had crooks on the back for our coats to hang
And a seat in the front for four of our gang

The kitchen table took pride of place
Where we sat for meals (we had to say grace)
Washing, ironing, cooking was all done on it
A clean cloth laid before we could sit

An open fire with an oven of metal
Chains in the chimney, to hang the kettle
An iron frame for saucepans and pots
A roaring fire soon boiled the lot

I remember the griddle cakes mum used to make
Had to have the fire just right, to toast not bake
She made a dough, as you would for currant bread
Rolled out and toasted the fire just red

Mum had to fetch the water up at the dairy house
With seven to wash and cook for, you never heard her grouse
She went milking twice each day, the money helped with the food
A mother in a thousand, I wish I was half as good

Dad was the Carter out in all winds and weather
Starting at 6 o'clock to get his horses together
He had a big garden he worked in by night
There was always fresh vegetables
Mum cooked for our delight

The house is there no longer, but the memories never fade
We were happy and contented, with love our home was made
Tho' mum and dad has long since gone, four girls still survive
When we meet, these happy times we talk over and revive

A F Childs

Notes

I was educated in Huntingdon, Knebworth and at Physical Training College, Bedford and Garnett Teacher Training College, London. I have worked as a Youth Employment officer, Personnel Welfare officer and have been a lecturer in Management and Business Studies.

I enjoy county tennis and hockey, golf (handicap 8), badminton, table tennis, ice skating and deck quoits. I won the Granada Silver Tennis Cup, given by the Granada Cinema, Bedford.

I have done a lot of voluntary work, as Lieutenant with the Biggleswade Girl Guides, the camp organising committee, Bedford, and the organising camp, Ampthill Park. I was treasurer for the National Council of Women for Watford and region, and was chosen to attend a garden party at Buckingham Palace.

For the last five years I have been permanently disabled and in a wheelchair (cannot walk) due to a car accident. I have partially blurred sight in my left eye and a lens implant in the right eye.

I live in a bungalow which I designed and had built by a builder friend, in Studham, Bedfordshire.

I have had twenty four poems published in books and anthologies in the last five years, since becoming incapacitated.

My poem is just a vision of a dream.

A Performance

Get ready to go out
And go to the loo about ten.
On to frame without doubt
In my wheelchair like an old hen.

In the hall don jacket
Then wheel my chair to inside door.
Stand up on frame and get
Across to the built up porch floor.

Front door I am then at
Here are two paving stones, one on
Top of other. Feet flat
Then help for lifting left one on.

Step on to paving stones
And over gravel. Then I touch
The open car door: Bones
Growing weary doing so much.

Hang on to the door, and
Swirl around. Sit on cushioned seat,
Feet given helping hand
Then hold on to the car, complete.

Ready for drive at last
Now on the open roads we go
Travelling not too fast
Enjoying every moment so.

Helped into wheelchair. Now
At garden centre to see the
Exotic flowers. How
Wonderful it all is for me.

Then lunch will soon be served
We sit at the table near door
To eat, drink; well deserved
I could not wish for more.

And away home we drive
After very long busy ride
Shall really just survive
On lovely memories, deride.

Gwendoline Albon

Newmarket

Notes

When my little horse, *Much Too Clever,* was weaned his mother was shut into the next field, but he opened the gate:- Hence his name!

It is Roses. Roses all the way
At High Haven Stables in Suffolk.
Spanish Beauty and Persian Maid
Perfume the air with their fragrance.
Little White Pet, Caroline Testout.
Pink and white, red and gold, tumble over
Fifty two stables festooned.
A glorious sight.

Just as lovely in comfort and care
Are the stallions and mares, fillies and foals
Housed in their boxes beneath.
'Much Sought After' has *winning* ways.
'MTC' is learning, much too fond of carrots -
and nuts.
'Darling Clover' one year old. Certainly *is*
in clover.
Pampered, petted, cosseted. More than any baby.

Trotting off to the Gallops in the Merry Month
of May.
'Much too Clever' is *very* pleased with himself
He is three years old today. *More Hay!*

Irene Brown

To my Twin Sister

Notes

I was born in Oswaldtwistle in Lancashire. My husband and I moved to Bath after the war. We have three children, two boys and a girl, and four grandchildren.

I'm going to try and write in rhyme,
Although it takes a lot of time,
I suck my pen in desperation,
And look around for inspiration.
First, I'll answer your curt letter
And see if I do any better,
But no, I know I never could,
Your verses are so very good.
Thank Kathleen for the card she sent,
I do hope she didn't spend the rent,
But had a good time in the brine,
With lots of fun, but not much wine.
Were Italians to her liking?
I met one once when I was biking.
Little Lynne will soon be ten,
She'll have many presents then.
I wish her many happy jaunts
Into the Chinese restaurants.
To school my children, have gone back
But wish that they could get the sack
They'd rather stay at home they say
Than be intelligent one day.
Dad and Grandpa, both are well
And that is all I have to tell.
Your twin is just the same as ever,
Loving, kind and very clever.

G E Yates

Country Style

Notes

I was born and raised in Hornsey, North London and now live in Chigwell Row, Essex with my third husband. We have five children and five grandchildren between us. The only baby left at home is a much-loved ginger tom called Ollie (named by me because of his obsession with food, he loves crisps and a bowl of spaghetti Bolognese).

I was born in 1946 and am a retired telephonist; for thirteen years I worked in the front office of a police station - needless to say, it was very interesting work. I also had my own tropical fish shop until my first marriage came to an end.

I have written approximately 150 poems to date, with many more in the making. They are on many different subjects, as I have been inspired by my extensive travels around the world and also by my own experience of joy and pain in the past.

My hobbies include gardening, writing, the theatre, dining out and listening to all types of music, from opera to modern pop.

My dream is to, one day, have a whole book of my poems published and I would call this Life, Death and In Between.

My poem, *Country Style*, was inspired by many lovely holidays in The Lake District.

I would like to dedicate this poem to my dear husband Mike for his loving support.

Country scenes with
panoramic views,
sheep in fields are
playing with the ewes.
Birds of many species
flying low
the pace of life in
country style is slow.

Sunday morning church bells
ring out loud,
the only time you ever
see a crowd.
In the church the
locals sit and pray,
and thank god for the
harvest of the day.

Home go farmers
wives upon their arm,
to have their lunch
then back to work the farms.
By evening when the work load
is complete,
the local inn is where the
farmers meet.
They talk about the pressures
of the day,
and sip their beer till
tensions drift away.
Then off they go to get
their well earned rest,
no doubt that life in country style
is best . . .

Pamela Jean

Notes

The idea for this poem came from a famous painting called The Scream. It shows a girl with her hands over her ears screaming. I think we all feel like screaming sometimes, I know I do.

Life is basically what we make it. But sometimes things can get that bit too much and we can't always see a way out, but we can often find a way out by just sticking with things and sometimes the unexpected can happen. That's what I think anyway. Life is full of good times and bad. Remembering the good times while going through the bad can help a lot.

This is the second poem that I have had published with Poetry Today, others being a college magazine and a local book called Oyez, oyez, oyez! It is also the first one I have won a prize for, which I'm really pleased about as I didn't think I was that good.

Untitled

I feel like screaming
Cause I feel so bad
Life is so hard
Too bad

I feel I'm stuck
Stuck in a rut
Life is so hard
Too bad

I know I'll survive
I'll always bounce back
Life is so hard
Too bad

Tracey Newman

169

The Peak

Notes

I was born in Coventry at the start of the war, during 1939. I have always been interested in the countryside and my garden, and during my schooldays I would write little scraps of poetry.

In the fifties I met my husband and took up hill walking in Snowdonia and the Lake District. I followed in the footsteps of Wordsworth. Then in 1989 I became ill with arthritis of the spine and could hardly walk. So depressed through my pain I could feel the cold and longed to climb and thinking of Wordsworth I wrote this poem. How I longed to climb to the top of a mountain once again, but as I wrote this poem I could see the beauty before me.

Now on my better days I can drive to the bottom of the hills and mountains and imagine I have climbed to the top of the peak and once again I see the beauty of the world around me.

Dedicated to my husband, Norman, who helped me to see the beauty in the mountains.

I climbed the mountain steep and bare,
But when I reached its peak,
Although the exertion came over me
The views there, I had come to seek,
Their beauty was unsurpassed -
The rivers, the valley green,
The blue skies overhead,
Wordsworth had trod this way,
Or that's what someone had said
And I thought of him as I went.
He must have seen this beauty
That gave him the gift to write.
With all this beauty around him
And his wonderful knowledge and sight
No wonder he found it all worthwhile,
If someday I could write an ode
Of all, the beauty that I've seen
I hope that I could put to words
Where Wordsworth may have been,
And pass it on to you.
So that you, like I will remember it,
The beauty that you seek,
The surprising happiness one may get,
When you climb to the top of a peak
And enjoy the views around.

P Baillie

Who am I?

Sometimes the impression I give
Of how my life I live
Can be difficult to understand
Without a helping hand
Even then it might not be
The real me.
Good old me so heroic
Always there always stoic
Always ready and willing
Kind, good and giving
There when a favour needs done
Laughing and joining the fun
Life and soul of the party
Strong, robust and hearty.
Not many have seen the other side
The one I seem to hide
Where my emotions lie
And every answer is why?

Joyce Inkster

Bottom of the List

Life is long looking back,
Just like a stroll on a cobblestone track,
The roads we walk, the streets we cross,
Memories are dense, like freshly grown moss,
    The laughs, the jokes, only to be absorbed,
    Wondering if, I was adored,
Circles of life rotate everyday,
If my body holds out, I think I'll stay,
For just a bit longer for something I've missed,
Extensions granted, by a medical list,
    I leap like a child, shouting Hip Hip Hooray,
    Shattered dreams, by another x-ray,
    The photograph states more black than white,
    Hi-tech machines can't put it right,
I lie in a room, silence is nigh,
Asking questions and wondering why,
Visions fading, up comes the sheet,
I'm not playing this game, Oh Lord I am beat,
    So, here I remain, laid on my back,
    Last thoughts of a cobblestone track.

Steve Lomax

Notes

I started to write poetry at the age of 18, having commenced nurse training, away from home for the first time, I was inspired to collect my thoughts and write them down in the form of poetry.

I have had four other poems published. The last one, *In Silence*, was published in *Rhyme and Reason* for Poetry Today. I am awaiting the publication of three more for Forward Press.

This poem, *My Son*, is dedicated to my eldest son, who has had many problems during his life. May he be given strength to cope and others the wisdom to understand.

My Son

In darkened corners of your mind,
You opened up, and there inside,
I saw the sadness that you bore,
The pain, you tried to hide.

Throughout your life, you've found it hard,
To be 'at one' with all you see.
Others have failed to understand.
You're complex personality.

Locked away inside yourself,
The thoughts and fears left unexpressed,
Alone, afraid of ridicule,
In being different from the rest.

The emptiness you hold within,
Has come to light, now that I know
The way you can't relate to others,
And let your feelings show.

But to me you do belong
My flesh and blood, you have done no wrong
The way you are, in being you,
Sensitive, caring, kind and true.

M E Rose

Lost Infants of Dunblane

Notes

I would like to dedicate this poem to all the bereaved families of the children of Dunblane.

Where have they gone
Why did it happen
They were so tiny
Never knew anger
Too little to understand
That the man standing there
With the gun in his hand
Has he come to join our game
Will he tell us his name
But he said nothing
He fired his guns
We thought they were toys
But he shot and killed
Sixteen small girls and boys
Our teacher is here with us
God brought her along too
Because with so many of us
Arriving all at once
He would not know what to do
She will take of us for now
And we like her so well
As for the man with the guns
He did not tell us his name
But for what he did to us
We hold no blame
He must have been sad
To behave so bad
In the end he came along
I think he knew
He had done a terrible wrong
Where he is just now
I do not know
But maybe we will see him again
And he will join in our games
He might find out our names
Then he will realise we all lived in Dunblane
We forgive him
Again we hold no blame

W Maclean

A Mother's Comfort . . .

My mother's black and hairy,
Her arms are strong and warm.
She holds me close, towards her,
To protect me, in a storm.

She brings me food and comfort,
And teaches me, of life.
I am learning how, to become,
A good man, for a wife.

Out here, in the jungle,
I swing from tree to tree.
With my friends, I chit chat,
Because I am, a chimpanzee!

Amber Roach

Notes

I was born in 1910, my home town is Stratford on Avon. I came to live in North Wales, on the Lleyn Peninsula, in 1966 and have been writing poetry, on and off, most of my life, mainly about birds and my animals. I have not had any published before now.

My daughter is an artist and lives on Anglesey.

Around the World

I have a little sailing boat,
Just like a proper one,
And I sail it in the rock pools,
And I have a lot of fun.

For when the sun is shining,
Then I go down on the sands,
And I pretend I'm sailing
Far away to foreign lands.

I'm sailing all around the world
Through sunshine and through rain,
But when it comes to supper time,
I've landed home again.

Sylvia Bryan

I am a 35 year old mum of six beautiful children and the wife of a farmer.

I really enjoy writing poetry as I am able to express feelings that I am unable to express openly. I have always been able to write poetry, since learning to write.

I enjoy needlework, especially cross stitch. I tend to knit a lot, as six children take a lot of time to look after and shopping usually involves too many problems. That's why I enjoy writing poetry, as I am able to escape from the noise and problems of today.

Country Life

The sun shines brightly
On such a lovely day.
Life is very peaceful,
In a funny sort of way.
Birds are flying all around
Nice and quiet, no heavy sounds,
Trees sway, to and fro,
Flowers blooming, everywhere you go
Yes, the country life's the one
For me.

M L Jones

The Garden

Notes

I am a middle aged clerical worker, married with one daughter and have lived all my life in Norfolk.

Nature inspires me to write some of my poems, with its beauty and harmony you cannot fail to feel the inspiration. I shut my eyes when recalling what I've seen, perhaps when reading this poem, you can do the same and actually be there, and blend in with the words.

Early morning, sun's beginning to rise,
Leaving for work, can't wait to feast my eyes,
Upon beauty and colour, each fair dawn,
Blues, pinks, recently mown lawn,
Each blade of grass, dew laden flowers,
Shining and glowing, for hours and hours,
All to share, marvel with awe,
Hearts are lifted, spirits soar,
Perfumes mingle, filling the air,
Wondrous, magical, beyond compare,
Eyes wander, marvellous view,
Beautiful gardens, for me and you!

Christine Russell

The Posh School

Notes

Everyone has a different point of view when someone in the family moves away from the accepted 'norm'. Behind the humour a bright child can cause much disruption in an otherwise ordinary family.

I want him to go to a 'Posh school'
Be a cut above the rest
(That's what my Mum says)
She sent in the application
Now I have to pass the test

You'll make him into a Nancy
Boys aren't like that round here
(That's what my Dad says)
The date is ringed on the calendar
It suddenly looks quite near.

You'll look so nice in a blazer
The uniform is so smart
(That's what my Gran says)
I'm revising my maths and English
Practising sports and Art

You'll get beaten up every Friday
Boys round her don't like a snob
(That's what my brother says)
But the name and address of a 'Posh School'
Looks good when I go for a job.

You did very well on your test, son,
Selection was really quite hard,
(That's what the letter says)
I start my new school in September.
My Mum had a cry in our yard.

Tomorrow I'm going to the 'Posh School'
I'm happy, excited and keen,
(That's what I say)
My Dad said, 'We're going to loose him!'
I really don't know what he means!

S Hall

Dawn

Notes

This poem is about my granddaughter, who has lived with me for most of her life. She's very beautiful and I love her very much, she is nearly 17. We share a love of the outdoors, ancient sites and animals.

I own 10 cats and a Jack Russell bitch who is nearly 13 years old. I show my non-pedigree cats and have won lots of cups and rosettes.

I had 3 poems printed in a small book in aid of an animal sanctuary, and one printed in a *Passage in Time*, for the International Society of Poets.

Moonchild, with hair the colour of moonlight,
And laughing blue eyes, the colour of a summer sky,
Do you know what gifts you hold at your fingertips,
And within your soul?
In harmony with nature, April showers
Like tears, fall softly on your cheeks.

In the prehistoric circle, you feel the
Power of the stones, as I do,
You stand on the earthworks
With a rainbow in your hair,
The stars put diamonds in your eyes.

The crystal swings for you, as it does for me,
We feel the same, we are woven together,
In an intricate web of love, light, and harmony,
The Goddess will protect us,
We are her daughters,
I know these things my child,
Because you are my granddaughter.

Sheila Giles

Notes

I am married with two teen-age children and have lived all my life in Blantyre. I work as a nurse and also trained as a midwife.

I have been writing diary-type stories and poetry, for over ten years, for my own pleasure and as a 'tool' to get my life in order. People, feelings and life events inspire me.

This poem is dedicated to my cousin, Margaret Duteil, who died in 1996 and whose courage inspired me to write, For a Down Day.

For a Down Day

When you search for inspiration,
And the going gets too tough,
Or look around for hopefulness,
And feel, 'I've had enough.'
Think of those who love you,
At home and far away:
And how empty would their lives be,
Without you there to say.

'Remember this, remember that'
The happy and the sad:
The richness of relationships,
To make your heart feel glad.

God wants you here on earth right not,
Your work is not quite done:
So heaven will have to wait,
To welcome another one.

Life is for the living,
Of which you are a part:
So embrace it in its entirety,
And lighten your heavy heart.

Dorothy Watson

Notes

I am aged 54, still single, but with many friends. Both my parents are in their eighties and still active. I have a brother and sister-in-law, a nephew, aged 29 and niece, aged 26. Both my mother and grandmother appreciated poetry - reciting it and writing it, respectively - so I believe their gifts have been passed on to me!

I was a teacher for twenty years, some eight years of which were spent in remedial teaching of children with learning problems. I found that they responded well to rhyming couplets, etc, collected from children's anthologies.

My interests include writing odes for friends' birthdays and recording my thoughts on the changing seasons in verse, but there are three other areas of leisure I enjoy: music, church work and gardening. After taking voluntary redundancy, from my job in a High Street store, I have decided to be self-employed, gardening.

I enjoy all kinds of music but prefer light classical piano pieces. I accompany a ladies choir, locally, and sing with them as a soloist. I also train a choral group at another church and am choirmaster and organist at my own church, where I have been a pastoral visitor for thirty years.

This poem was composed in the Staff Room of the local high street store where I worked. There was a spate of untidy Saturday staff who were not accustomed to leaving the room clean and tidy. It left a couple of early-bird Monday-Friday members frustrated having to wash a sinkful of crockery and cutlery before working in the stockroom. Eventually my poetic efforts were worthwhile as senior management decided to arrange a rota to share the responsibility.

Tidy Up ~ Please!

There's a phantom about! Beware!
Full ashtrays choking the air
As we sit to contemplate
Do we *have* to tolerate
    Such a mess?
    What distress!
And, what makes the tidy ones forlorner
Is that person who leaves in the corner
Cups that have dregs of coffee or tea.
How long does it take for the remedy?

Please will you do your own washing up?
Rinse with hot water each mug or each cup,
Saucer or plate and cutlery too
Don't leave it for someone else to do!
And don't merely leave 'em on one side *to drain* -
Wipe and replace in the cupboard again.
Only the ashtrays go in the left-hand drawer;
In the right, knives, forks, teaspoons galore,
Kitchen utensils in orderly fashion;
Or someone, one day, in a fit of passion
Will throw everything up into the air
In utter despair! Does nobody care?

It can really make a saint quite bitter
To see such unnecessary litter!
For bins are provided and constant hot water
Please remedy this . . . and do what you oughta!

John Rolls

A Poem About Thinking Too Much

Notes

I have only recently begun to write poems, which tend to come into my head when I least expect them.

My poem about thinking too much was inspired by many long afternoon walks during a summer living in the Peak District when I would ponder on life!

My ambition is to write and illustrate a series of children's stories and verse, whilst making yummy cakes and owning a teashop.

Sometimes my brain
will not shut up
and makes me think
about things too much.

It makes me consider
things in my head
which are too hard
for me.

When I think about things too much,
about life and sheep and bottoms and such,
people think I am all funny
cos it makes my words go all runny . . .

Rosalyn Stewart

The Doctors

Notes

I am 27 years old, I was born in South Wales but now live in Drayton, Oxon. I've had one other poem published, entitled *The Sea.*

I enjoy writing, travelling, motorbikes and parties.

I *dedicate this poem to my brother, Andrew and my niece, Georgia.*

Today I went to the doctors,
I always think it's a terrible place.
There's the old man coughing in the corner,
And the boy with the zits on his face.

The woman's waiting there for ante-natal,
She's three months gone you know!
And it's all happening inside her tummy,
The baby is starting to grow.

The nurse is giving injections,
It's the three in one this week,
And the little lad's face goes crimson,
As he lets out an almighty shriek.

Now the telephone rings,
The receptionist answers,
And you've got to be clever to get past her.
She asks you your symptoms,
And tells you what to do,
I'm sure she thinks she's the doctor.

I'm getting quite worried,
I've been here for an hour,
And up until now I've been ignored.
Don't they understand that after ten minutes,
I get thoroughly cheesed-off and bored.

I've counted the cracks in the ceiling,
And by now I'd been there for ages,
I'd read the Woman's Own, Woman's Weekly and Titbits,
And now I'm half way through the yellow pages.

Over the tannoy a voice booms 'Lewis,'
And my face always turns pale,
As I hobble towards the doctor,
I start to perspire,
It's just me now and my ingrowing toe nail.

Stephen Lewis

Kate (Pub Dog)

Notes

Jean Tibbott, born in Oldham Lancashire, now lives with her husband, Keith in Southwaite, Cumbria. They both enjoy wine tasting as their main hobby and, since retirement, painting with watercolours.

Poetry writing started as a form of therapy on losing a well-loved cat. That first poem *Our Kate* was published in *Northern Voices* during 1995.

Kate (Pub Dog) was written the week that this boisterous boxer dog died. She was loved by all the locals and it was hoped that in some small way this poem would help her live on in their memories.

The clientele of the Southwaite Arms were greeted one and all
With a friendly bark, a wet nose and a dropped toy or ball.
This was 'Katy' wanting to play and everyone joined in,
When visiting darts teams came along it usually helped us to win!

One day, a young lady came into the bar
Mini-skirted up to her thigh
Old Kate came behind her, wet nose twixt her knees,
A young man got a black eye!
Dear Kate, I'm sure, had a rare sense of fun
She seemed to grin all the time
And everyone laughed (except the young man)
He was accused of the crime!

There are lots of these incidents fixed in my mind
Of how Kate was loved by us all
We'll miss her wet nose, her wiggle, her bark,
And it's sad she won't come when we call.
But dear Kate will be there in that pub in the sky
Waiting for people to greet,
So do not despair, though it may be some time
Inevitably we shall meet.

Jean Tibbott

The Test

The test was long and hard with
the questions and my answers
trailing my arms.
I looked long and hard and said
the questions over and over in my mind,
but nothing seemed to work that
day when my mind went *blank!*

Amanda Corbett

The Wind

Notes

I am also having another poem published - *A Dreary Day, The Jigsaw* by the International Library of Poetry. I have had a short poem published a few years ago - *Lost Love* by the Parnassus Magazine of New Verse.

Where does the wind come from?
Where does he go, he's had such fun today
He's blown my washing off the line and over the wall
I had my hair done, oh what a mess, bet he had a laugh
He's blown over the hills and out to sea
He blows the ships against the rocks
Does he have fun doing that.
Now where has he gone?
He'll be back be sure of that.

E M Hayes

Time

Notes

I have been happily married for over twenty years and have spent the last seven years living in Peterborough. I have two teenagers and work with children in a school setting.

I was prompted to write this poem one day when I heard about a relation of mine who had not got long to live. I knew that because of this, how precious time was to all of us, and, that we should make every moment count and not just waste the time that was given to us, as, we do not have long on this earth and never know when we will be called to another plane.

What is time, how come it flies so fast?
Where does it come from, where does it go?
Why does it never stand still?
So we can capture each moment.

Time is to be enjoyed, if you can savour,
Savour the best times and enjoy to the full.
Spend years, months, days, hours, minutes, seconds,
Filled to capacity, brimming with life.

Time never stands still, always moving on
Sometimes it goes quick, sometimes slow
But, it's always around, forever creeping on,
Tick, tock, tick, tock on and on.

What's happened the clocks stopped!
Is that my internal clock or the one outside
Quick, it needs to be bump started,
As I know, that time has not yet run out.

Since time is precious and too short,
Make each minute of each day count
And live to the full,
So no regrets when your time has gone.

Bridget Taylor

Notes

I would like to dedicate this poem to the teachings of the native American people.

For them each incarnation into the physical world was to walk the Good Red Road. On that journey through life, they saw the earth and all the creatures that walked or crawled or flew, as expressions of the Great Spirit, as too were the trees and plants and even the very stones themselves. They walked a Road of Wisdom that mankind could learn so much from today.

I would also like to thank my mother and father, Doris and Bill Nye, for all the love they have given me - a love that has helped give me the courage to hold my head high and walk my talk on My Good Red Road.

Red

What do you see when you see red?
Anger, aggression, the lower chakra,
Stop lights that always make you late?
I see poppies in the summer
And perfumed roses by the garden gate.

You see bank accounts in debit
And lots of bureaucratic tape,
I see holly berries at Christmas
And the furry lining of Santa's cape.

I see the colour of dawn's rising,
I see the feel of the western sky,
I see the colour of fresh-picked strawberries,
I taste the richness of a cherry pie.

When you see red you're in a fury,
Of all the negatives red can be;
I see the colour of my blood
That circulates round all parts of me.

I see the colour of a passing people
Whose legacy has stood the test of time.
I see the road that I am walking,
I see the grape that makes the wine.

You see the colour that maddens a bull,
You see the colour the matadors use;
You see the colour of a body scarred,
You see the colour of a short fuse.

I see the colour of a ruby crystal,
I see the colour of carnelian,
Scarlet and magenta
And of course vermilion.

I see the colour of molten lava,
I see the warmth of a fireside glow,
I see an amazing beam of colour
That's first on the lips when you sing a rainbow.

Gill Alzano

Do You Remember?

Do you remember?
It seems so long ago
When we lay 'neath the trees
And cherry blossom fell like snow.

Do you remember?
Once 'pon a time I guess,
When no one could part us:
Long lazy days of happiness.

Do you remember?
When I kissed your sweet lips?
Heaven! and time stood still.
Coming in were our ships.

Do you remember?
Halcyon days gone by
When we were so in love,
And there wasn't a cloud in the sky.

Do you remember?
When we ran fleet of foot?
But we arrived too late
And the door was already shut.

Do you remember?
I can see you do not.
But my memories remain,
For to me you meant such a lot.

Where have they gone?
Just dreams one supposes,
But then I shall never forget
Those nights of moonlight and roses.

J Millington

More of Life's Little Lessons

Notes

Love, honour and obey: I did - this is the result, otherwise I wouldn't have bothered.

Written in seclusion as a dedication to, and to escape the rantings of, my dearest Honour, wife, dearest companion and chauffeur, who drove me to drink.

I am a poet and peasant: a retired senior citizen of Geordie roots and heart, who loves the hobby of making home-brew consumables. I produce a weekly audio tape of radio and television programmes for local blind, sight-impaired and script-denied people.

Be tall, be tall, but not so tall
That height prevents you hit the ball.

Be quick, be quick, but not so quick
That haste prevents you take your pick.

Take heed, take heed, this quest I plead
'Flowers grow in heaven, but does the weed?'

Be heard, be heard, you must be heard
So speak out loud when you spread His word.

Make haste, make haste, and don't delay
Today's the morrow of yesterday.

Be drunk, be drunk, but not that drunk
You cannot rise from where you've sunk.

Be old, be old, but not that old
The reaper begs your hand to hold.

Be high, be high, but not that high
You rise above the kite you fly.

Be lost, be lost, but not so lost
Before you're found folk count the cost.

John A Moore

Dunblane

In a corner of Scotland a million tears fell
Dunblane was visited by the devil from hell
Do roses grow there anymore
Is it spoiled forever by Satan's spore
Do people smile in this tainted place
Is it forever a sorrowed place
Or will God reach out His loving hand
And bring back peace to a troubled land.

Andrew Stevens

Notes

I am 59 years old and live in Leven, Scotland. I've always liked poetry and started writing poems a few years ago. As I am now severely disabled and in a wheelchair I have plenty of time to write.

This is the third poem I have had published. I'd like it dedicated to the precious children of Dunblane, forever in our hearts.

Libra Baby

Notes

I am Pearl Powell and live in Freshbrook, Swindon, Wiltshire.

My other previously published works include: *Lost Love* (International Society of Poets - 1996) *The Other Side of the Mirror* awarded editor's choice for outstanding achievement in poetry; *Drunken Man, Joyrider, Return of Spring, Magic of Winter* (Anchor Books - 1996 and 1995); *Schoolboy, Evening into Night, Waterfall to Sea* (1996, 1995, 1994); The International Library of Poetry, semi-finalist in 1996 international amateur poetry competition; *My Fair Lady(A Lasting Calm)*, due to be published summer 1997; *A Cry of the Flower Seller (Poetry Now South 1997); Life's Clock (Poetic Fever)*, due to be published March and April 1997 by Poetry Now.

I started writing in 1993 and it is my favourite pastime. I am fascinated by words and I get inspiration from scenes, paintings and photographs. My personal ambition is to publish a book of poetry on various themes. My other interests include music and travel.

Golden hair beauty, not yet two
You have lost another shoe
Replaced one last week, now despair
Money tight, not a dime to spare
You gurgle, smile, without care
Throw building bricks, from high chair
Squeal and laugh, with great delight
When you give me another fright

Entered my life, late in September
Rained all day, I well remember
When you entered, that rainy day
Sun came out, clouds rolled away
Brought me joy, great love untold
Change you not for rich man's gold
Wealth have none, but rich indeed
Have you baby, to bounce on knee

Into your bedroom at night creep
Watch you quietly while you sleep
Love you always, I promise you
Whatever great world, to you do
May I always, with you be
Watch you grow, your beauty see
God watch over you through night
Keep you safe in morning light

Golden hair beauty, you're my ace
Egg all over your small face
More on floor than on plate
For my appointment, must be late
Proud I am, you are mine
Show you off all the time
Keep you always, my sweetheart
Pray the lord, we never part.

Pearl Powell

Notes

I started writing poetry about seventeen years ago, although I never took my own poetry seriously. I would sometimes show it to family and friends. I thought it was essential to have a great mastery of words, but I realised, through reading so much, it is very individual and now I write from what is within myself, (but I always keep a dictionary by my side).

I like reading and gardening but, most of all, I love going for walks, when I seem to get ideas for poems more easily.

I dedicate my poem to my dear dad, (Bob) Robert William Bradford, who passed away 21st January 1997. I will always love you dad. I also dedicate this poem to my mum, (Marge) Margaret Jean Bradford, who I am so very happy to have for my mother and I cherish her with all my heart.

Chocolate Box World

I live my life on a chocolate box
In a hazelnut whirl
I am the girl on the toffee tin
With a sweet expression and curl

I drift in and out
Of rose-covered cottages
Pretending that I live there
I picture myself, sitting by the fire
In some big old rocking chair

Escape as I must from a plastic world
Where things seem so ugly to me
Just those who I love
Live in my chocolate box world
For it's there that I am so
        Happy

Christine Bradford

Mother of Mine

We start our lives as babies and feel our mother's love
She will show how much she cares for us, like we were heaven from above
When we have grown from cradle and nappy
She *will* always be there,
And if we can make her happy
Anytime, anyplace, were.
And so dear mother, *I'm saying*, though its not always face to face,
And many a time you have put me in my place.
But now that I'm older, I can only see
You did everything and gave the world to me
And looking back now, because I have so much time
I am so very glad, mother, God made you mine.

Rosemary Cleaver

Notes

I am married to Doug, we have one son, Marc and one step-daughter, Michelle. I work as a checkout assistant at a busy supermarket quite near to where I live.

My first poem was published when I was twelve in the church magazine. I am attending college to gain more qualifications. I am also a school governor.

The inspiration for this particular poem came from a friend, she felt her mother was giving her a hard time.

Sadly, my mother died when I was five.

Notes

I was born 9th May, 1934 in Oldham and educated in Devon and Liverpool. I have two sons and three granddaughters and live with my little dog and foundling canary, quite near to my family.

I enjoy countryside walks, classical music, Haydn especially. In fact I love all the Arts.

I worked as a registered nurse from 1974 until 1994 when I retired.

I began to compose my poetry in June 1996.

My Feathered Friends

Come on tiny garden birds
Sing for your morning meal
Let's keep the magpies from our door
Don't give them chance to steal.

Little robin pecks the seeds
A flock of sparrows too
Here's my all-time favourite
A tiny tit of blue.

Blackbird and his mate arrive
They're happy digging roots.
Raven's dine across the field
Joined by noisy coots.

We'll fill the feeders full again
For they'll return for tea
Plus nets of nuts for tiny friends
All beautiful, wild and free.

At dusk all settle in their nests
Or bird house in the tree
Tomorrow is another day
For feathered friends and me.

June Henthorn-Mather

Teacher's Helper

Notes

I am a retired secretary, divorcee, with two married daughters, five grandchildren and an elderly mother who was widowed when I was six years old.

I became a born-again Christian in 1993.

Writing poetry was one of my hobbies as a child and in my teenage years. In recent years I have been inspired to write poetry to celebrate family events, or school events for my grandchildren. I am also inspired by the beauty of God's creation in flowers, trees, streams, hills, cloud formation, little children, elderly people and animals.

My granddaughter came home to ask her mum
If into school she would come
To help the teacher was her request
Grandma said she'd do *her* best
The Access course took up Mum's time
So Grandma she did step in line
Rucksack, baggage and walking boots
On the school trip they all took
What a lovely healthy sight
Those young children on the hike
To the Three Shires' Head they walked that day
Then on to Gradbach YMCA
Not a murmur of discontent
At the long day they had spent
As round the table they all ate
Supper followed by chocolate cake
Then after that they all washed up
Every plate and every cup
When ready for bed they all did look
The teacher read from a story book
The next day started with a pond dip
Quite the highlight of the trip
The children looked with eager faces
Whilst teacher pointed out the places
Where, if they all would carefully look
They'd find the insects in the brook
I'm glad I had the time to spare
To help the children in teacher's care.

Jean Collins

Happiness

Happiness is food
Happiness is Jesus
Happiness is Everton
winning the Premier League Cup,
Happiness is holidays
Happiness is toys,
Happiness is gogos
Happiness is birthdays.
Happiness is Christmas
Happiness is Marc Bolan
Happiness is all other sixties
and seventies music.

But Happiness is Paradise.

Robert Old (8)

Words

Notes

I was born in Hillingdon, Middlesex. I'm married, a housewife with two daughters and one son. I'm now retired and a pensioner. I was educated at state schools and left at fourteen, without qualifications, to go out to work. I'm the eldest of nine children: four brothers and four sisters, my parents are deceased.

My hobbies are knitting and letter writing, some of my letters have been printed in newspapers, as well as some poetry. I began writing poems during the Gulf War, at the request of a family friend, and have continued writing seriously ever since. My poems are based on everyday life and circumstances.

I live in a village outside Milton Keynes. There are beautiful views from my windows, overlooking the fields, and I can see for miles.

I love photography and I have many albums of photos, both of family and places we have visited over the years. Very many are of steam traction engines; we used to go to steam rallies but no longer do so. Some snaps I took in Battersea Festival Gardens in 1952 / 53, one is of a young Bryan Forbes and other stars. I often wonder what they would say if they knew I had them.

There are words for many occasions,
Whatever they may be,
Words like 'Congratulations',
'Love' and 'Sympathy',
When 'Retirement' means a parting,
'Good luck in all you do',
'Best wishes for the future',
These words sincere are true,
Words can recall a memory,
Hidden in mists of time,
Brought back again from its slumber,
By a verse of beautiful rhyme.
For those who are sad and grieving,
There are words to ease the pain,
Special words of comfort,
That will not be said in vain,
So always choose your words with care,
In everything you say,
For words are easily remembered,
As we go along life's way.

M James

Notes

Born in Port St Mary, Isle of Man on 8th February 1912, Noel Williamson is married to Phyllis Bernadette and has five sons and one daughter, 18 grandchildren and 18 great-grandchildren, to date.

He has been retired since 1977 and regards poetry and darts as his main hobbies.

He has been writing since his last year in the RAF (1950). His writings have been mainly influenced by experiences and certain news items. He was awarded first prize in the Hertfordshire Circle Literary Competition in 1972, for an anthology entitled *First Forty,* and recently, with a certificate of commendation for his poem, *World Unity,* by The International Society of Poets publication in the anthology *Voices on the Wind* 1996. He has a total of 500 poems to his credit, a number of which have appeared in magazines and anthologies, and has been nominated as a distinguished member of The International Society of Poets.

He has compiled several anthologies including; *The Poetry of Darts, Hertford Castle and Other Poems, Manx Poems, Poems for the Young (And not so Young)* and *Out of the Darkness,* (Christian poems).

All Out For Fitness! was inspired by an earnest desire to re-attain that enviable state, and, therefore, dedicated to all those who wish to make a similar effort!

All Out For Fitness!

Am I becoming stout? - Yes, sir, without a doubt!
Must cut potatoes out! Also, cut butter out!
Beer - can I do without?
Better keep quiet!
Cut out the 'eating out', reduce my diet!
Make the effort all out!
At least, I can try it!

More and more exercise - that would be very wise,
in moderation - dangerous, otherwise!
Hope to reduce the size of my posterior
and corporation, waistline and thighs!

Try to develop muscles not lately used -
those that have been abused, or just neglected;
that's what it's all about,
fitness respected!
Not as it used to be, almost rejected!

Then I may possibly reduce my middle -
moving around with ease,
using up calories,
not get so out-of-breath -
fit as a fiddle!

Noel Egbert Williamson

For Gwendoline

Notes

I was born to a farming family in January 1944. When young I wasn't much bothered about the farm, but I felt at one with the fields and open spaces.

I attended a convent school and married a farmer in 1965: we have two sons.

I have many interests, my family being my first love, gardening a close second. Gardening has led to travel which, in turn, has introduced me to many friends. I enjoy photography, and many forms of art; cooking for family and friends gives me great pleasure. I am thrilled by words spoken or written.

We went to Bournemouth
A few years ago
At night we went
To see how far the sea would go
The air was crisp
The night was clear
The stars shone bright
We were happy there
In that holiday seaside town
We fed squirrels and pigeons
On the ground
Some say I was telling a tale
But at night I heard a nightingale
We listened to music
From the bandstand
Folks in their Sunday best
My, they looked grand
We've heard songs from hilltop
And deep in the vale
But none so sweet as that nightingale

Sally Masters

The Mobile Phone

Notes

I am employed at a department store in Royal Leamington Spa, where about ten years ago, I wrote a poem which was printed in a magazine. Then, in 1992, I wrote a humorous poem, entitled *The Demon Drink Machine*, when we had one installed in the store. This was published in a book of poetry.

Mainly my poems are about people I know, when they get married, retire, emigrate, special birthdays, etc. Just for fun.

Now have you walked along the street?
The place where lots of people meet.

And suddenly you hear a ring.
Whatever is it? Ding, ding, ding.
The mobile phone of course.

And shopping in a busy store
You're loaded and can't carry any more.

And suddenly you hear a ring.
Whatever is it? Ding, ding, ding.
The mobile phone of course.

In church a wedding is being held.
It's enough to make you go cold.

And suddenly you hear a ring.
Whatever is it? Ding, ding, ding.
The mobile phone of course.

The vicar says 'Repeat I will,'
And Grandma rings about a bill.
She gets the time of wedding all confused
The congregation are not amused.
And travelling on the train one day.
So peaceful, what a lovely day.

And suddenly you hear a ring.
Whatever is it? Ding, ding, ding.
The mobile phone of course.

The conversation went like this.
'I'm on the train don't bother me.
No, he cannot come to tea,
Unless he gets his hair put right
I would rather he kept out of my sight.'

And walking round the farm one day
Not mad cow disease, dare I say!
And suddenly you hear a ring.
Whatever is it? Ding, ding, ding.
The mobile phone of course.

The farm hand carries one about
So Farmer Giles can check him out.
With pigs, sheep and cows to feed
And also planting lots of seed.
There's not much time to stand and stare
Or go to sleep. Would he dare?

Now if I do the lottery win
I will buy a mobile, what a sin.
And then will join the ring, ding, ding.

Betsy Taylor

Notes

I was born in Shropshire on 13th June 1980 and have lived in Mid Wales ever since. At present I am a member of Newtown High School's sixth form, studying GNVQ Leisure and Tourism.

I enjoy writing and I write poems and stories about almost everything, from visiting a friend in North Yorkshire to feelings and thoughts. My other interests are collecting memorabilia of my favourite pop groups and writing letters to my penpals.

To date this is my second poem published with Poetry Today, and my third poem to be published altogether.

I would like to dedicate this poem to everyone who has to suffer the pain of losing somebody close.

Missing You

I sit by your grave
And weep sad tears,
forgetting the world around me
Forgetting my fears.
Remembering the times
we once had,
all of the memories
both happy and sad.
I'm missing you
And I wish we could be together,
Someday, it'll be me and you forever.

Nikki-Ann Trow

Memories

Memories of babies laughing and crying,
Memories of parents sick and dying.
Favourite places to gladden my heart,
Memories of families wrenched apart.
Memories of hopes and terrible fears
Continue to haunt me over the years.
Music drifts through the air,
Easing my loneliness and despair.
Memories of a love that never blossomed
Less painful now but not forgotten.
The arms that once held loved ones near
Are empty now through the lonely years.
The loveliest of memories linger in my heart,
Together in spirit yet always apart.

Hazel Grant

Notes

I was born on 18th October 1937, in Northfield, Birmingham. My parents are Frank and Lily Connelly.

My published work has been mainly Christian verses, though I do enjoy writing more light-hearted work and some are published in various magazines and anthologies.

I am 60 this year and look forward to retiring, in Blackpool, where I now live.

Daisy

I was once a little girl - many moons ago
I remember playing with a flower white as snow.
It had a tinge of red and a yellow centre pad.
Everywhere I found it growing made my heart glad.

Little daisy you grew with abundance all round,
You gave me happy hours playing with all I found.
Daisy chain, daisy chain, gave me such fun.
I placed you round my neck as I played in the sun.

I would wear my daisy chain with pride all day
As off to the park I was taken to play.
I would climb the slopes of lush green grass
Then roll back down them and into friends crash.

Alongside my sisters and friends I would play
My daisy chain a-top my head they would lay,
As I became their Princess of the Day.
Whilst their dancing figures would twirl away.

Little daisy, little daisy, I am adult now and so
I dare not into the park and a daisy chain grow.
Too grown up to wear a daisy chain anyhow
Just a sweet childhood memory you must remain now.

Maureen Connelly

Notes

I am 62 years old, retired and live alone. I have six children and ten grandchildren aged between nine and twenty five.

This if my sixth poem to be published - all in the last year. I wrote a lot after the death of my husband in 1962 but kept it private - it was a release for my grief. A great comfort to find I could express my feelings in this way. Then I didn't write anything for twenty years or so and suddenly started again, but only verses to personalise birthday cards and such. I was too busy working and raising my family.

Now it is beginning to surface again. I cannot explain it. If I think of a subject suitable for a poem nothing happens. Yet suddenly, out of the blue, I feel the words just flow and have to grab a pen!

That's Life

I've often wondered, wondered why
We were put on earth - to die

In such a short, short span of years
Some spent in joy, but some in tears.

Some men have left their mark behind -
Remembered for deeds to all mankind.

Deeds of courage, which live on
After they themselves have gone.

Some wrote books, poetry too,
Trying to teach us what they knew.

But we must make our own mistakes
And learn thereby. But it always takes

A life's span to learn life's teaching
Then we're gone - there can be no reaching

Back to tell what we have learnt
To those who follow, who wish we weren't

Gone beyond recall.
Where's the point of it all?

Irene Miller

Notes

I am 48 years old and I live in a hostel in South London. I had one poetry book published in 1993, called Hippy Fred's Poetry Book. I sang in a recording studio in 1979. I like listening to music. I have been writing poetry for twenty years. I have schizophrenia and arthritis.

Junkie's Dilemma

What was I doing
All those years?
LSD and whiskey
And countless beers.

I must have been mad
And it made me feel bad,
I must have gone crazy,
They thought I was lazy.

When I was young
I took pills by the ton,
Even at the factory,
It wasn't me.

Stoned every day,
I should say,
But what did I achieve,
Everywhere I lived, I had to leave.

Not reading,
Heart and soul bleeding,
Living for the pills,
Just for thrills.

In the sixties
All the hippies,
Incense and marijuana,
Beatles and instant Karma.

I can't believe it,
Body destroyed,
Senseless confusion,
Total disillusion,

Now I'm alright,
I can sleep at night,
Ten years older,
Body getting colder.

I gave in
And learnt how to sing
And acting normal,
But my brain was small.

We live and learn,
We grown up to earn,
I should have realised
What it meant
To be a junkie.

Frederick Lewis

Notes

I am originally from London but now live in Lowestoft, a seaside place, which is in Suffolk and I love it here.

I love animals and have six cats all different colours. I also love gardening but I only have a small one, although it has plenty in it.

I have written a few poems about the environment, as I do buy all natural things and do my best to look after it.

I am a Christian so I do write a lot of Christian poetry, I do not work as I am not a well person, so I do get a lot of time for reading and writing, which I love.

Many of my poem have been published in poetry books. I started writing poetry a few years ago but my first poem was published in May 1995, so I now have about 58 published.

I enter poetry competitions, therefore I have to keep writing a lot of poetry every week.

Certain things and people in my life inspire me to write, like this particular poem, which I wrote many years ago.

Beauty of the Lady

When my days are lonely
And I sit alone
I look at the picture on the wall
That hangs inside my home.
The beauty of the lady
Who sits inside the frame
Makes me wish it were me
But I'm just plain Jane.
Sometimes I dream it's me up there
And everyone who came would stare.
I know I must wake up from this dream
But it's been nice being a beautiful queen.
Now it's back to being plain Jane
But deep inside I'm the lady in the frame.

Linda Roberts

Darkness

Notes

I am 58 years old, a house-wife, living in Bath. I have recently lost my husband, who was totally blind, in March 1996. Two months previously to this we lost our pet dog, Shelley, who was 14½ years old.

Since my bereavements I have felt very lonely and vulnerable and have been trying to relay some of my feelings through writing poetry.

I have written another poem entitled *Love is Like a Raindrop* which is being published in the spring. I am also entered into a prize draw which takes place in March 1997.

Your world was full of darkness
Things of beauty you could not see
You could only imagine the colours
Or the swaying of the trees
Things like flowers
Birds flying high above
You could not have existed
Without the greatness of my love
Together we conquered obstacles that came
But without you my darling
Life will never be the same
There is one consolation
I have within my grief
Now you are at peace
I know that you can see

J M Pollard

Live for Today

Notes

I am aged 62, retired and have one daughter and four sons. I was born and bred in Looe, in Cornwall, where I have lived all my life. I come from a very long-existing respected Looe family, my maiden name being Pengelly.

I have been writing poetry for a number of years, off and on, but never entered any in a competition. One of my sons entered one of my poems in an international amateur poetry competition; my poem made the semifinals and is published, which prompted me to send my work to you.

I wrote my poem *Live for Today* because my thoughts on life is - to make the most of it, to think about tomorrow and not worry about the past, being true to yourself and most of all to remember the best things in life are free.

My hobby, apart from writing poetry, is swimming and I love singing; I sing in a ladies' choir in Looe and sing solo.

My family is very special to me and it is especially nice for me to see them and their families gathered together, all happy and well, as at Christmas.

Live for today and new tomorrow,
Yesterday's gone with its joy and sorrow,
Think of the future, but remember the past,
And let the happy memories last.

Strive to be happy, be good and true,
But don't let life make a fool of you,
Work hard so you may enjoy your play,
Treat others right as you live day by day.

You will be hurt sometimes and sad,
But your heart will be true and you'll be glad,
So be yourself, take off the mask,
And live each day as if it's the last.

Ena Eastley

Accident Prone

Notes

I am retired, born June 27th 1935. My enjoyment in poetry is to write about life's happenings around me, and life as I see it. I write about people, nature and pets.

I have had three poems accepted by The International Society of Poets, in three anthologies, one accepted by Poetry Now, and this one by Poetry Today, all since November 1995.

My hobbies are knitting, writing poetry and country music. I am a Southern Country reporter for the two clubs we go to. This is my second marriage: I have four grandchildren of my own and 12 step-grandchildren. My husband's name is Dave.

I was over the moon to know this poem had been selected for publication and also that it is a prize-winner. My third poem which was accepted by The International Society of Poets, has been selected to go on an audio tape, Sound of Poetry. I will continue writing and hope my efforts will give as much pleasure to others as I get from writing.

Wherever I go, whatever I do,
This tale of mine, really *is* true.
Taking a shortcut, in heavy rains,
I fell over pub courtyard chains.
Getting up, and rubbing all down,
Bruises, breaks, and bumped crown.
Black and blue, I ache like h...,
Always believing in doing things well.

Many people do call me a pest,
My accidents *do* cause some jest.
Falling in my garden, just recently,
Got the biggest black eye, you ever did see.
Although not rich, I enjoy good health,
Really believe, in some fun myself.
My bumps and bruises, make me groan,
From being so *very* accident prone.

June F Allum

Notes

I was born in 1941, Mavis Helen Whitaker, one of two children, have two married children and four grandchildren, and now work part-time as a receptionist.

I have written many poems, but only recently have I had the courage to let other share my secret thoughts.

I have had two other poems published, Dreams and Parting and the inspiration for these and this poem, Evening, my latest, I get from secret thoughts and memories of a lost love.

I now live alone in Oakworth, West Yorkshire in the heart of Bronté-land where I am trying to write my first story.

Evening

Now evening comes
And shadows creep
Along the mossy bank
The light is gently fading now
As silence spreads about
Only quiet footsteps do I hear
No other sound around
I look toward the crescent moon
As she gazes down on me
The rocky path seems lonely now
As daylight now has gone
The trees wave gently in the breeze
And beckon down to me
It seems as if they want to hear
The secret thoughts, I keep
Within my lonely heart
But as a tired sigh I give
A secret smile I show
Tomorrow is another day
Who knows what joys it brings
So lock away those thoughts for now
Within my broken heart
And sleep until the morning light
To wake again with hope

Mavis H Whitaker

A Lesson for All Who Manage Others

Notes

I live by the sea in North Wales, with a view of the beautiful Snowdonian mountains.

I have been trained in massage and health and beauty therapy, so various aspects of healing interest me.

I have an abiding interest in nutrition, movement and self-healing. I also enjoy music and dancing.

I began writing poetry as a school girl, and have continued off and on.

I am concerned about how people communicate with each other, and feel the lack of it is one of the main causes of the problems in the world. Because I believe communication is very important in the work-place, I was inspired suddenly to write this poem as I was getting ready for bed one night. It was particularly for the Housekeeper of a local hotel where I was working, at the time, as a cleaner.

Please, *tell* me what you want me to do.
That's how communication will work for you.
If it isn't clear, we'll be in a mess.
It isn't wise to think I will guess.
Presumption's a game I will not play,
I'll surely get it wrong that way.
And disappointment you will find
If you expect me to read your mind.
'Tis a lesson to learn and must accept,
Disappointed we'll be if we expect.

Violet Marsden

Notes

I am 61 years old and live in South Devon during the winter. However, being a caravan site warden for a national club, I spend my summer months on the Lleyn Peninsula in North Wales.

My poem tells of the different, but important stages in my life from five years old in the London Blitz, through formative years in rural Yorkshire up to my present somewhat nomadic way of life.

Sounds is the first of my *Five Senses* project, all to be written in the theme of my life's experience.

Sounds

Sounds are part of the fabric of life
From birth they are with us both day and night
As children we hear them, then store away
The feelings they brought for another day.
Now that I'm old I have time to recall
The sounds of adventure that I chose to befall
In a war-torn city with low-flying planes
Bombs and guns bringing an end to my games.
The sound of a binder, harvest time as a boy.
Brought a smile to my face, pleasant thoughts to deploy.
The noise of the playground and chalk on a board
The end-of-day bell, then my spirits soared.
So to work where the din was intense
Learning, improving, then some things made sense.
Joining the navy, hearing sounds of the sea.
Is this really where I wanted to be.
Meeting a girl, her voice was so bright.
Separating was awful, noisy trains in the night.
Parting was constant, making me blue.
Until the day I heard the words 'I do'
The cries of my children, the laugh of my wife.
Sounds of the family bringing joy to my life.
I look back on life and hear those evocative sounds
Echoing through time, my happiness abounds.

Brian Downing

Ode to Estate Agency

Ten little house buyers thinking the market's fine
one has lost his buyer though
so now there are nine.

Nine little house buyers - house hunting they hate
one has changed his mind now
so now there are eight.

Eight little house buyers - will they go to heaven
one has damp and woodworm
so now there are seven.

Seven little house buyers - will a sale they fix
one is now divorcing
so now there are six.

Six little house buyers looking for a dive
one didn't like the colour scheme
so now there are five.

Five little house buyers becoming now a bore
one is made redundant
so now there are four.

Four little house buyers chasing a cheap fee
one has bought in Hampshire
so now there are three.

Three little house buyers with agents now to woo
one hasn't got a mortgage
so now there are two.

Two little house buyers looking for some fun
one has stressed out completely
so now there is one.

One little house buyer out there on his own
we can only hope and pray
he finds himself a home.

Tessa Winston

Theatre Trips

Notes

I am a retired social worker, married, with a son and daughter and five grandchildren. I still do some voluntary work and I enjoy reading, walking with our dog, going to the theatre, doing cross stitch and pottering in the garden.

I started writing poetry about three years ago when I became a senior citizen. It suddenly seemed that my thoughts and feelings wanted to be expressed in poetry.

Since then I have had several poems published in various anthologies and I reached the final of the 1996 International Society of Poets' contest.

I dedicate this poem to my theatre going pals who add to my enjoyment of my theatre trips.

To the theatre I'm off,
Dressed up like a toff!
It's all such a thrill,
I can't get my fill.

To the station I hurry,
In such a flurry,
My friends to meet -
We must find a seat.

The journey is fine,
Swap their news and mine.
We arrive on time,
Pleased the weather is fine.

A browse round the shops,
The sales are just tops.
A sandwich and a bun,
Then the moment has come.

The show has begun,
Oh, what joy and what fun,
The music that thrills me,
The emotion that fills me!

Back to the train,
The memories remain.
I must come again -
Again and again!

J Scarisbrick

Mouse Chorus

Notes

I am married with two teenage children, and my interests are drawing and painting, reading and writing stories. I have written six stories for children which have been accepted for publication, although this is my first attempt at writing poetry.

I hope my poem, *Mouse Chorus*, will appeal to both adults and children alike.

My eye was drawn to a strange beam of light,
As I gazed through my window, one cold winter's night.
The snow was falling steadily, but I just had to see,
So I crept down the garden as quiet as can be.
I followed the strange light, and as I drew near,
I stopped just to listen, for I thought I could hear
Whispering and giggling and talking in hushes.
So I crept very quietly and peered through the bushes.
I wasn't prepared for what next met my eyes,
And I stepped back in fright, and gasped in surprise.
For a party of mice had gathered together,
In bonnets and scarves, dressed up for the weather.
There were small mice, and tall mice
And young mice and old
But all dressed up snugly to keep out the cold.
I counted the creatures, there were twenty or more
And each held a hymn book in its silvery paw.
One mouse had a lantern, its light shone so bright
And encircled the creatures in a halo of light.
Then they struck out in chorus, it sounded a treat.
With voices enchanting, melodious and sweet.
And all I could do was gaze in awe,
At each bright eye and tiny paw.
And as I watched and listened, the more I was bewitched,
By those furry little creatures, with whiskers that twitched.
Then one old mouse who looked very wise,
Peered over his spectacles with beady black eyes.
And seeing me peeping, gave the alarm.
The mice scampered away, though I meant them no harm.
That's so long ago now, but on each winter's night.
I gaze through my window, to hope I'll catch sight
Of the quaint mouse chorus, that once gathered there
And to hear their sweet voices ringing in the air.

Shirley Wood

Isolated Thoughts

Notes

Jenny is a 22 year old student from Drumbeg, in County Antrim. She is currently completing her final year at the University of Ulster, studying Communication, Advertising and Marketing. As well as writing poetry and short stories, Jenny plays the violin, guitar and piano, and sings with the Belfast Philharmonic Choir.

In particular, Jenny finds inspiration for her writing from nature and creation.

I dream of being a wanderer, gazing forever
at the outside world. Ignored by all-
labelled, mocked and scorned yes,
but left alone . . .
Separate from the throngs
hurrying onwards,
pressing forward in time.
They have somewhere to be,
someone to meet -
all at some decided time.
They have notes and coins,
cars and clothes
pressing engagements and mansions . . .
but I would have freedom in myself
and would lack nothing,
I'd wander aimlessly, enjoying life
and I'd pause to drink from it and savour it . . .
Yet with a strange twist of 'sense' I'd feel
that with only pennies in my pocket -
I'd be better off then they.

Jenny Halliday

The Tale of Terrible Teddy

Notes

Born in Birmingham fifty one years ago I have four children and eight grandchildren.

I like to write poetry with a religious or spiritual message.

This poem was penned after hearing on the news of children who kill, seemingly for 'fun'. I got to wondering why and Terrible Teddy was born. Could it be the same for these sad children?

Terrible Teddy was naughty and bad
Yes, Terrible Teddy was quite a lad.
He tore his clothes, broke things to bits
Was always throwing tantrums and fits.
He punched other toys who lived near by
Then one day Daisy Doll said 'Oh Teddy why?
Why are you always so naughty and bad?'
And then she discovered poor Teddy was sad.
No one had shown him the right way to play
How to be kind and loving and gay.
No one had ever given him a hug
They'd just left him alone, there on the rug.
So Daisy she kissed him and gave him a squeeze.
'But there must be no more fighting Teddy please,
I'll be your friend and I'll always be there.'
And Teddy just needed someone to care
From that day on, he has been good as gold
Now that he has a hand to hold.
We all need love and we all need care
And always to know someone is there.

Valerie Lloyd

I'll Never Settle for Second Best

Notes

I became interested in poetry during my school holidays. I was asked to write a composition on how I spent the time, I often won a prize.

In later years I wrote the lyrics of an occasional song as, after leaving school, I went into theatre land as a song and dance entertainer for many years.

I married in 1960 and after several years I had to care for my husband, a very sick man. I am now a widow and a pensioner.

I'll never settle for second best
When I'm sure there's better on the way
I won't wait for spring to name the happy day
Romance is in the air, so what do I care.
I just won't settle for a little short and fat
They drive one up the wall, like a fussy cat
I like my man to be mature, wise and tall
There may be dark clouds around
Where there's very different tykes to be found
I'll never settle for second best
If I can't find the best.
He may not be tall, dark, and handsome
But if he's kind, understanding and loves me
I'll look no more,
       I've found the best.

Eva Rusher

The Eskimo

Notes

I am sixty eight, a retired mathematics lecturer, living near Morecambe in Lancashire.

With a life-long interest in literature, I have been writing poems for some thirty years; originally sonnets and serious verse, lately lyrical and comic verse for my grandchildren.

This poem was written for Cory who is adventurous and fascinated by things mechanical.

In Greenland lived an Eskimo;
Tan Tarkin was his name.
His house was made of frozen snow,
His diet Arctic game.

As a boy he'd learned to fish
Upon the frozen pond.
But all the time it was his wish
To see the world beyond.

What lay beyond the ice-clad slopes
Which stretched towards the sun
Was the spring of all his hopes
For future years to run.

With wife and family to provide
With fish and fur and walrus hide
He mastered all his tribal skills
In hunting and communal kills.

One day a strange and noisy bird
Descended from the sky
And men with accents yet unheard
On Tan's world cast an eye.

Tractors, trucks and giant drills
Appeared among the lakes and hills.
Tan was dazzled by the sight
In mechanics he proved bright.

He learned to drive and to repair,
Studied hard and showed great flair
And would, in time, it was quite clear
Make a first class engineer.

Tan now travels far and wide
And carries out his job with pride.
But he still loves the ice and snow:
He's still Tan Tarkin, Eskimo.

T Day

Notes

During World War II, as a teenager, I joined the Women's Land Army and was sent to work on a farm in Oxfordshire. It was really the most beautiful place I have ever seen, and the source of the River Cherwell which flows eventually into the Thames.

The farmer and his wife were both wonderful people and I think this was the happiest time of my life. I have always looked back on the farm as my 'spiritual home' and it has been the inspiration of several of my poems.

In Search of Peace and Quiet

What a noisy place the countryside
Is turning out to be!
With barking dogs and plaintive sheep
And the cuckoo in the tree.
With farmhands driving tractors
And the neighbours sawing wood
I am going back to London
And there I'll stay for good!

Doris Ginsberg

Summer Nights

How swiftly bright Apollo flies,
How suddenly the fair day fades.
But stealing softly, dusky shades
Spread beauty over earth and skies.

I love these, dreamy summer nights,
With their romantic twilight hours.
Blooming on high are starry flowers,
And moonbeams gleam like fairy lights.

Gay-coloured clouds sail up above,
The nightingale sings, all night long.
A breeze accompanies his song.
This is the perfect time for love.

Your sweet embraces are a part
Of the strange rapture night-time gives.
Here, fine poetry breathes and lives.
I fold its magic to my heart.

Pauline Ransley

Why is it Always Me?

Notes

I am 48 years old, married
with two grown up children
and I live in Devon.

I have had one other poem
published but have only recently tried to get my work in
print, although I have been
scribbling for years!

I enjoy painting and drawing
and I am interested in gardening and nature. I love
dogs and have been working
with Guide Dogs for the
Blind, as a puppy walker, for
the last four years; I have
been prompted to write a
number of poems through
my experiences with these
pups.

Why is it always me?
That does all the jobs around the house
That cooks and cleans
And helps the spouse

There's shopping to do
And letters to post
I really don't know
Which job I hate most

'Oh where are my tights?'
Is my daughter's woeful cry
'I washed them this morning
And hung them to dry'

Son's just come in
'Mum could you just
Press my clean shirt?'
'Well if I must'

If I decorate the hall
I still wash and clean
When there's work to be done
There's no one else to be seen

If ever I rest
The doorbell rings
And nobody knows
How to deal with these things

It seems I'm complaining
I do that then smile
The moans make it bearable
At least for a while.

Lynda Burton

An Elf Called Mischief

Notes

I suppose I was about four years old when I first began to put words together. I lay awake at night, making up rhymes about the man in the moon sailing away amongst the clouds.

Periodically, during childhood, I used to put short poems together but never kept them. Actually, I was too busy trying to keep up with the bottom of the class. Not, I'm afraid, succeeding very well.

When my son was about eighteen months old, I wrote a poem about him and put it into a book. From then on, I wrote more and more. I love both poems and stories. I get immense satisfaction out of it. Luckily, my brain is still quite active although I am now starting my twilight years. I hope I will be able to carry on for a while yet.

He wrapped his arms around himself
And chortled loud with glee
That cheeky little impish elf
He turned and winked at me.

He waved a circle with his hand
And folk turned down side up
They bounced around upon their heads
And balanced on a cup.

He danced around and in and out
And pointed here and there
All sorts of things were happening now
He was grinning like a bear.

He waved folk here and waved folk there
And made them do all sorts
He certainly enjoyed himself
And poured them all some ports.

He stacked folk up like a load of bricks
And built up quite a wall
And then with glee he pushed them down
He was having quite a ball.

He worked himself up into a tiz
Then suddenly felt tired
So he curled up into a ball
And slept as he desired.

But just before he went to sleep
He suddenly remembered
And with another wink at me
He righted all dismembered.

So if you seek folk acting queer
Just take a look around
Your bound to see that mischief elf
Just lying on the ground.

Joan Vincent

To My Son

Notes

My name is Cynthia Turner, I am 60 years old and come from Deal in Kent. I am married with three children and five grandchildren.

I first started writing poetry about ten years ago, after the death of a very dear friend. I was feeling guilty that I hadn't seen her often enough. I can only write about things that affect me deeply.

My other hobbies are playing the piano, gardening and going to the theatre.

I'm sorry I've not much to offer you,
No talent or worldly acclaim,
No money or wealth or position,
I tried but all was in vain.

To give you the start you deserved in life,
But I failed with material things,
The only thing left is oh so much love,
You can have all of that with no strings.

I tried to teach you the good things of life,
Like truth and compassion and trust,
Like honesty, fairness, a laugh and a smile,
To have a good life they're a must.

To say you're the best thing that's happened to me,
Is the understatement of all time,
That here in my life you were destined to be,
I'm so very proud that you're mine.

And now that you're older and flown from the nest,
To make a new life for yourself,
Don't ever forget that my love is still here,
It can do so much more than just wealth.

It can help dig a garden and paper a room,
It can show your new wife that I care
For her just the same as I still do for you,
There's more than enough you can share.

And as time goes by and you watch me grow old,
And I change and don't seem the same,
Forgetful and grumpy and stiff in the knees,
In fact an out and out pain.

Remember that inside this body so frail,
Is the love that will go on and on,
Until the time comes when we have to part,
I'll never stop loving you son.

Cynthia Turner

Wishes Answered

Notes

I became a born-again Christian after the death of my eldest daughter. I started to write poetry about the same time.

I am a senior citizen and enjoy gardening and cooking. I am a member of the Ebenezer Baptist Church in Cwmbran.

I have had several poems published in different books.

The sheer beauty of the hills that surround my home.
Thro' those peaceful vales I feel so free to roam.
To see the sunset sink behind those tree-lined hills
To walk along those woodland lanes where the wind is still

The warm sun casts its dancing shadows upon a quiet path.
Those light rays send their messages to stir a Welshman's heart.
I worship this beautiful land, this land is home to me
To be as free as those wild daffodils growing by a man-made sea.

The beautiful fields who's carpet is so refreshing to the eye.
They are watered and refreshed by the spring rain that falls from the sky.
Those gentle streams are brimming with those rainbow coloured fishes
The heavenly landscape gardener has answered a Welshman's wishes.

Those wild daffodils gently lift their trumpeted heads to blow a song
This is the land of Harlech, this is where my spirit belongs.
Thro' those hillside valleys I am given so much freedom just to roam
To admire the sheer beauty of the hills that surround my home.

J F Grainger

Notes

I am 16 years old and currently studying for my Highers - Music, German, Modern Studies and English - at Boroughmuir High School in Edinburgh.

I love all sports and music, and play the violin, piano and oboe.

I have previously had one poem published and was very happy that this too was accepted for publication.

Although not a proper tennis player myself, I love to watch it on television, especially when Wimbledon comes round each year. I will be found glued to the television for hours.

1995 was a great year for many at Wimbledon and while enjoying the action, I decided to write about it. From the first line, the ideas just seemed to flow.

I would like to dedicate this poem to Katherine, a very good friend of mine, who, on numerous occasions has tried to teach me to play tennis. It will take me a long time yet, but thanks to Katherine for being so patient.

Tennis at Wimbledon 1995

The stroke of the ball
The grace of it all
The crowds cheering
They can't believe what they're seeing.

The powerful play
Gets better each day
The big strong serve
Everyone gets what they deserve

The greats in the men's singles
Watching them makes you tingle
The points rapidly change
But some shots are out of range

Sampras goes without a hitch
As do Becker, Agassi and Ivanisevic
They look so elegant when running around
When Agassi wins, he kisses the ground

Sampras won the trophy
Graf won the plate
Will they win again next year
And win Grand Slams to date?

Sheena Macrae

The Eternal Song

Notes

I am 75 years old, living in Birmingham and have written poetry for my own amusement since I was a child, but only recently offered any for publication. This is my second poem to be accepted.

I dedicated it to my husband Arthur, who, with a wild stretch of the imagination, is the heavenly being who rescued the sparrow from the clutches of our large Persian cat called Montague.

I am happy and singing my little song
As I fly from the hedge to the ground,
The sky is blue and the sun is warm,
There is plenty to eat all around.
When suddenly from nowhere the monster springs,
All fur, muscle, teeth and claws,
I remember the warning too late it seems,
As I shiver beneath its paws.

My song is forgotten, I hear myself cry,
As the feathers are torn from my breast.
'Tis a nightmare, a shock and a horror,
And I wish I were back in my nest.
Why must I die? Oh! it's very unfair
That my life has to end in this way.
'Dear Lord of the birds, hear a little one's prayer,
Let me live, if it's only a day.'

In the midst of my terror I hear a great shout,
Someone witnessed the dastardly deed.
A heavenly being just gave it a clout,
And the monster has gone with all speed.
As the being looks down at me from above,
I huddle there, shaking with fright.
With my feathers all wet and bedraggled,
I must look a deplorable sight.

A warm hand, so gentle, tender and kind,
Descends, holds and lifts me right up.
Just like a nest, I know I am safe
As I nestle inside its cup.
It holds me so quiet, peaceful and still,
Till my pounding heart trembles to calm.
My feathers grow drier, my legs gather strength
From the power within the palm.

The being and I know the time has come,
I am ready to fly away,
His fingers unfold to let me go,
I am free, but I long to stay.
'Goodbye, dear friend whoever you are,;
As I soar swiftly up in the blue.
'I can sing my song again, as before,
But I'll sing it only for you.'

Marjorie Jenkins

Freedom

Notes

I am 25 years old, married to Richard and have a seven year old daughter, Jade. I live in Saffron Walden, Essex and I work with horses.

I have been writing poetry for six years and have had two other poems published.

From here I see freedom
Their wings stretched out with the clear sky behind them
Where are they going?
Do they have any worries?
Looking down on us what do they see?
They have families, each other,
So do we.
But this is reality,
The freedom of their lives is a dream.
A dream I long for
Oh, to be a bird and fly!

Joanna Stacey

Notes

I was born in 1929 and have been a book-keeper all my working life. I have been married 45 years.

My reason for writing poems is to help eliminate the pain I suffer from osteoporosis.

I was born in London but moved to Lincolnshire in 1995 for a peaceful environment.

A Moving Poem

The year was nineteen ninety five
'Twas getting harder to survive, so
We left our dear old London town
For pastures new to settle down
Well after sixty seven years
We both just shed some little tears
Of course the two of us had no doubt
Whatever came we would stick it out
So our dreams came true
Just around here
Where we now dwell
In Lincolnshire
Of course the journey
Was not easy
In a heavy six wheeled 'Luton'
Well we had to get a 'move on'
'Twas journey's end
When midnight struck

At last we had made it
And given some luck
It took six months to settle down
No bother, no fuss, not even a frown
It's summertime now, flowers in bloom
Oh yes! We have a garden now too
Green grass from room to room!
We have found some new friends
Some are the feathered kind,
Magpies and robins, doves and jays
Starlings and blackbirds
And warm summer days
I know we will be happy here
A walk on the sand, a stroll on the pier
Yes we will settle down here too
We even have a lovely view
But we are *not* far away
So if you cannot call us today
We will call you.

B Clark

What is a Carer?

Notes

You have always been a carer and had quite a lot to bear, to look after your baby sister when your mother wasn't there.

It meant you couldn't go out unless she went with you, remember you were only nine and she was barely two.

Since then you've cared for our four sons and done everything you could, it's through you love and care they ended up so good.

Now you still look after mother who's eighty five years old, but it's one thing after another that the years will take their toll. So now is the time to take a rest and start to live again, remember you have done your best and your caring not in vain.

I dedicate this poem to my wife Daphne.

What makes someone a carer?
You're never born that way
To look after someone else
Every night and day

So what kind of carer would you say
Someone who's special in every way
A person that smiles through thick and thin
One who carries on and never gives in

They never ask to have a day off
And they also never have pay
They just get on and do the job
In a happy sort of way

There are many kinds of carers
Like the ones that just pop in
To find out if you are alright
And if you be needing anything

So would you like to be a carer?
With no life of your own
Being at someone's constant call
And always staying home

That's why they are very special
And take things in their stride
By looking after a dear old friend
With lots of love and pride

And when that dear old friend has gone
And has left you on your own
Who is left to tend to you
There's only the nursing home.

Peter J Hurdle

Notes

I am Les Croft, 50 years old, and born in London. Married for 28 years and now reside in St Just-in-Penwith, Cornwall.

I have been writing and rhyming for thirty months and hope to publish my own anthology in 1997. I have had thirty poems published to date, and have been given recognition from the following; International Society of Poets, together with commendations from Rhondda Community Arts, Meridian Poet and Writer Club 1994 and 1995, followed in 3rd prize in the winter of 1996.

As this is my second publication with Poetry Today, I should warmly like to say thank you to all that have encouraged me to take up poetry seriously. As a person with little sight, even writing can be difficult.

Finally, as a tribute to my dear departed father, Leonard, and my mother, Vera, who is 80 years old in May 1997, I dedicate this poem, for without them, I would not be the person I am today. I thank them with all my love.

Food For Thought

Food is on the table
Eat it while it's hot,
Stop what you are doing
Or you know for what.

Slaving at the oven
To make the mealtime right,
Warm the human innards
To stave the cold of night.

Meals are meant for sharing
Good for one and all,
Build strong bones and fibre
Healthy, fit and tall.

Les J Croft

The Day You Died

Notes

Inspiration was when I was in a depressed state after my husband, Bernard, died unexpectedly.

The words flowed from deep inside me along with the tears.

I felt so lost and alone even with my family around me. He had always been there. It helped the pain I felt to write. We were married for 45 years.

Well my love you did it and on the thirteenth too,
I bet you were surprised
Yes my love you went to sleep,
A sleep so deep you will not wake again
I am so lost and lonely,
My only happy thought is that it was not you left behind
With an 'oh' so deep ache within,
Please wait for me my darling for the day - I too will sleep.
Only to wake to your smile
For I know this day will come
When, I do not know! My love lives on - till then.

Irene B Finn

Weeping Willow Tree

Notes

I'm 32, live in Yorkshire and am a housewife. I have two children.

I started writing poetry when I came out of hospital, a few months ago. I am inspired by nature and events going on around me.

Weeping willow tree flow
freely over me
Take my hand and say
come and play

Come and play some
day with me
We'll smile again
at the weeping
willow tree.

Anne Tatchell

Shoes

While idly passing the time it amuses me,
Observing shoes on the feet of people I see.
Awaiting a train at a London Main-line station,
I watch the hurrying, scurrying shoes of a nation.

Some are with eyelets threaded with laces,
Others buttoned or strapped, all going through their paces.
High heeled and low heeled and trainers galore,
Familiar designs from a Marks and Sparks store.

Toeless sandals so comfortable and light,
A boon to corn sufferers easing their plight.
Now seated in the train, I gaze across the aisles,
At the motionless footwear of various styles.

All come in pairs, a left and a right,
Like two close companions keeping each other in sight.
Oblivious, the wearers are miles away,
Immersed in the papers and the news of the day.

If they knew of the thoughts that my mind invade,
I'd be carted off by the white-coated brigade.
To continue my shoe thoughts - where spent they the night?
In wardrobes, on shoe racks, or under beds out of sight?

Or slung into corners arousing dismay,
When they seem to go missing the following day.
Now they mingle closely with others of their kind,
All carrying out the daily grind.

In various directions they will journey today,
Some on short distances, others far away.
A few may travel on the great jumbo jets,
Others tread around parks with owners walking their pets.

Maybe those trainers I see across the aisle,
Will soon set off jogging mile upon mile.
The expensive black leathers with shiny toe-caps,
No doubt they belong to executive chaps.

So here's to our footwear, be they trendy or staid,
They will always be part of life's cavalcade.
Shoe manufacturers can sleep easy at night,
Always in business for shoes left and right.

Mary Tevlin

Notes

As far back as I can remember I've been venting my inner feelings in verse; from anxiety, angst and anger, to amusement, amazement and amorem!

Willing, or sometimes unwilling, recipients of these verses have been as diverse as the feelings expressed; from friends, family and confreres, to enemies, opponents and bureaucratic institutions, particularly the misnomered 'Benefits Agency'.

Spare Ribs was written for my friend Shirley, who had the misfortune to crack some ribs last year. I hope it was not too painful for her to laugh!

Now approaching my dotage, I continue to find and record the funny side of life in verse.

Long may this state of affairs continue.

Spare Ribs

Adam was dissatisfied
When *God* gave him a rib for bride
Then *Eve* 'snaked' off
and hurt his pride!

Said *God,* 'Though it might make you sore
From twenty ribs I'd make a score
of brides for you, if you want more?'

Adam groaned and said, 'You dope'
With twenty brides I could not cope
Sans ribs to cage my lungs,
                I'd *choke!*

Sheila Allen

Notes

I am aged 65, but was forced into earlier retirement due to ill health. I am a former local government officer and computer operations manager. I live in Sale, Cheshire, and have a tabby cat, called Kit.

I am interested in words and wrote my first poem, *Streetlamp* as an exercise in rhyming, about eighteen months ago. *Nature's Awakening* was my first published work.

Streetlamp

Twinkle, twinkle little light
Shining in the street so white
Through my window, O so bright,
I cannot get to sleep at night.
To Council I don't wish to write,
(One might as well go fly a kite!)
And I'm not looking for a fight -
Yet from my home I'll not take flight.
To try again, I thought I might
So closed my eyelids very tight,
Soft music played, sleep to invite,
But still those rays my eyes excite.
If I could climb up to that height
I'd break the lamp with great delight,
But I might get a nasty fright
When I attempted to alight!
Yet still that beam does me incite,
And now I'm fearful for my sight;
It doesn't seem to be quite right -
Can no one save me from my plight?

William A Yarrow

Notes

I am a 50 year old widow
living in suburban Dublin.
My hobbies and interests include: reading, music, art,
cookery and walking.

I have been writing since the
age of 15 and my inspiration
comes from scenic views,
events and people.

The poem is abstract and not
connected with any event or
person.

Free Will

Walk on the water
Walk on the moon
If it will mean
You will be there soon
Hush do not
Chide, stem the tide,
And with me abide.

Bernadette Levy

239

Youth

Notes

I have had a second chance to love and to be loved. I have been writing poems for fifteen years - something comes to mind and away the writing flows, mostly just about everyday thoughts and events.

When I was young I roamed the hills
Because then I had no ills
I had neither ache nor pain
And didn't care if it did rain

To school each day I had to go
Walk through the rain and through the snow
For the lessons I had no heed
Education, I saw no need

The water-butt it was empty
And I had to carry plenty
The cows too they needed milking
Plenty of time to do my thinking

Each week it was a long long time
When I was young and in my prime
For the dancing I would long
Even if I didn't know the song.

Now time is like a racing track
And I cannot hold it back
Of my life few years remain
But I can't go back again.

A J McHenrey

The Stag

Notes

I was born Kathleen Reece and lived in Grimsby with my three sons Darren, Jamie and Christopher. I have now re-married and live in Market Rasen with my husband Adrian.

Living in the countryside and having more time on my hands inspired me to write poetry. I have written several poems and had a few published. *The Snowman's Tale* was very highly recommended and short-listed for Poet of the Year to which I currently received a special commendation certificate. I am, at present, writing my own book.

I love animals, and own one dog, two cats and two ferrets.

There he stands six feet tall
with his magnificent sounding call
above the herd his antlers show
casting shadows in the snow.

In the distance not far away
a pack of dogs are having their day
a day to hunt, a day to thrill
men on horses hunting to kill.

Horses galloping over open ground
the pack of dogs running round and round,
sniffing here and sniffing there
holding noses in the air.

The dog in front, with head held bent
suddenly discovers it's on the scent
rushing forward to horns that sound
goes the thundering horse and hounds.

The stag leads its herd through hedge and mires
bravely rushing through barbed wire,
he knows their lives are all at stake
as he takes them to a safer place.

When the noise all dies down
he knows this time he's won the round,
he licks his wounds he's done his task,
let's hope this is the very last.

Kathleen Tutty

A Lottery Win

Notes

We all dream of winning the lottery. These are some of my thoughts - but if I was to win the big one, I would love to give up work and spend my time writing more poems and short stories, and maybe one day be a famous author.

My dreams are not reality,
Nor will they every come true,
But listen very carefully,
And I'll share them with you.

I do not wish a small house,
No, mine would be quite grand,
And if my dream allows me,
Maybe an acre of land.

My garden would be elegant,
With trees of many kinds,
Shrubs flowering all year round,
The pleasures are yours to find.

The house would be a masterpiece,
But still very cosy and neat,
In every room a real log fire,
So I can warm my feet.

My two faithful companions,
Would always be at my side,
But what I would call them,
This I've yet to decide.

So that is some of my dreams,
There's still so much to say,
Maybe I will be a winner,
On some cold and wintry day.

But for now I keep on dreaming,
Of my lover and of my home,
My companions by my side,
And places I've yet to roam.

Lucy Lockett

Number III

Notes

Dorothy Dennis is now in her eighties. She was first introduced to poetry when a small child at school; she can still recite with enthusiasm and affection the quantities of lines from Longfellow's Hiawatha, which she was asked to learn.

During her later years, she has composed many poems - usually during times of dejection and melancholy, but sometimes in a sense of celebration and gratitude.

After all the fun and laughter
I'm thinking of you tonight
And wondering if you enjoyed your stay
Was everything all right?
The rooms seem lost and lonely
The beds are empty too,
The shoes and cases have all gone
Your smiling faces too,
But come again my sweethearts
I'll look forward to that day
Bring back those shoes and cases
Once more with me to stay.

Dorothy Dennis

Gaby

My little dog is sleeping
Beside me on the bed
All covered with her blanket
I can only see her head.

She's snoring very softly
Her little eyes shut tight
Her steady breathing soothes me
Through many a sleepless night.

Her little tummy rumbles
And she shuffles on the bed
Opens her eyes and wags her tail
So I stroke her furry head.

She stretches out her little legs
And gives a contended sigh
Then off she goes to sleep again
Knowing that I'm nearby.

And in the morning when It's light
And I open sleepy eyes
I see her gentle friendly face
Lying by my side.

Paula Vance

Notes

I was born in 1935, lived in Shakespeare country, Stratford-on-Avon, through my childhood. I am single and live alone, but enjoy the friendship of many.

I have had five other poems published: *Home, Over the Hill, The Dove of Love, What is a Friend.* and *Life.*

My hobbies are: dressmaking, knitting, playing piano, songwriting and of course writing poetry.

Not having very good health, I find writing poetry very relaxing. I just get an idea, think about it and a poem goes down on paper.

Go!

Why has my go got up and gone?
Why am I feeling so low?
Why do I just want to keep in the shade,
When I used to be all of a glow?
I'd like to be full of vitality,
Like I know I once used to be.
But now, that is just a thing of the past.
Even thinking seems to beat me!
I'd think of all sorts of things to do,
And do it I would with gusto.
But now, if the chance of something comes up.
I'm afraid the answer is just, 'No.'

The heart is willing so you have a try.
But the aches and pains make you want to cry.
So, when your go has got up and gone,
You just leave it to others to put the show on!

Anita Bricknell

Notes

I am 54 years young and my name is Cynthia. A mother of four children with 13 grandchildren. I re-married eight years ago and I have a stepson, Aaron aged 10, who has lived with us for the past six years. I work in a hospital, as a health care assistant, in the care of the elderly.

I started writing poetry a year ago and now have a collection of just over 100 poems which cover a large span of subjects. Just about everything inspires me, especially people. I went back to night school when I was 48 and got three GCSE's.

I wrote this poem after looking at my pay-slip one month. I thank my husband and friends for their support.

Pay Day

It's that day again
Money for this, money for that.
Will I have enough to buy that new hat?

Ever ending bills that say
This must be paid for today.

Can I rob Peter to pay Paul?
Soon I will have no money left at all

One day I just hope that I can see,
Some of my pay-packet left for me.

C Britton

A Child's Face

Notes

I am 58 years old and have three children and four grandchildren. I live in London and have recently had to retire from my work as a nursery nurse due to illness.

I can't say when I started to write poetry but I have always been able to make people laugh with my humorous verses in birthday cards and such.

This poem was inspired partly by another, written by Dorothy Low, and called 'Children Learn what they Live' and in my nursery, I saw many expressions on children's faces, from smiles to tears. Being a multiracial nursery, I found that all children have the same emotions and express them in similar ways. I miss being there with them and occasionally drop in to see them!

My hobbies are handicrafts and Crystal Palace Football Club and fishing.

When I look at a child's face
I see sunlight
When the child smiles
I see trust
When a child is laughing
All the world melts and troubles
dissolve into dust

When I look at a child's face
I see sorrow
When the child frowns
I wonder why
When a child is crying all the
world cries and hardens and
troubles pile up high

Make a child laugh
Always try to smile
Walk a straight path
And in a little while

The child will be grown up
With children of his own
And all the laughter you have
had, and the joys that you have known

Will make your child laugh
And hopefully he'll live
Without much sorrow in the world
And learn to take and give

A child's face is a world of
information. Look and you will learn.

Carol Taylor

Sixty

Anne M Frost (nee Griffiths) born 26th December 1930, Brierley Hill, Staffordshire, the eldest of seven children. I started school aged 4½ years and had a wartime education with no special qualifications, (but always in the A stream). I left school aged 13 years and started work one month later then aged 14 years. Joined the HM Forces at 18½ years as an assistant cook in the WRAC. After six months transferred to QARANC for nursing and posted overseas to Suez, Fayed and Moascar in Egypt where I gained an Education Certificate 2nd class. I married overseas and have seven children and I am a grandmother. I retired as a nursing auxiliary at Christmas 1995.

No writing experience, my poem, *Sixty*, is dedicated to my sister June in a special book for that particular birthday in July last year. Another poem, *The Teacher*, was printed in the book *Rhyme and Reason* in February 1997. Small verses were written for family and friends, for special occasions, for handmade cards. One poem, *Climate* was entered for a competition in September 1996 and has reached the semi-final and will be in the final in the spring 1997.

My hobbies are dancing, competitions, art, yoga, reading and I had a painting in the mid art exhibition in 1993, and a further painting to be exhibited 22nd March 1997.

Now you've reached, the big *'60'*
Time to reflect -
On what you know,
You have come a long way -
With great education!
Don't be sad, you should be glad;
You can always take a short vacation -
Think what you'll gain,
You'll find a new life -
Start over again,
Without stress or strife!
You can give of your all,
And not be at everyone's beck and call,
New things to do,
More time for you!
Not giving up - just starting anew,
And you won't have to race -
Take life at a slower pace;
Then without more ado,
You'll come smiling thro:
It will be a great day -
On your special birthday!

Anne M Frost

I am 37 and married to Steve, we have two children, Matthew aged 10 and Claire aged seven. I am an RMNS but have not nursed for eleven years due to a back injury.

I started writing poetry as a teenager to express in words the feelings and emotions I felt inside. As I grew older, poetry was a release for my anger, pain and confusion when faced with a traumatic stage in my life. This included the death of both parents, many operations, one recent one for cancer.

Since I have married and had my children my poems now reflect the joy and happiness I have found.

Memories of Us was written in 1982, it was a poem written for lovers by a lover. The only thing that is important to lovers is what is happening at that moment in time and the future is a lifetime away, therefore irrelevant, until you are left alone with just your memories!

Memories of Us

Dawn breaks, her warm fingers brush my face
the way you always did when we awoke
But she doesn't make me feel the way you did
We would lie, maybe not even touching
but knowing if we wanted,
the feelings of love, warmth and security was there
All we had to do was reach out, touch,
and hold our bodies together as one

Night comes, with the moon,
Casting a silvery beam into the darkest corners
the way you did with your smile, laughter and love
into the darkest moments of my life.
But she doesn't brighten my nights the way you did
You would tell me of the things you would do
the places you were going, and the freedom you would have
I felt alive and excited to be so much a part of your plans
even if, only as a listener

And then we would make love
both knowing how much we needed each other then,
and not thinking of the time when
the day would break, and the nightfall
When we would not see them together

Elizabeth Mitchinson

Why do People Have Dirty Habits?

Notes

I am 59 years old, married to Andrew, who helps me a lot, as I am house-bound and in a wheelchair. I have two daughters, one son and five grandchildren, with one more on the way. I have two parrots and two dogs.

I was born in Cannock but now live in Crook, County Durham.

Why do people smoke?
That is a dirty habit.
You burn your money,
Oh what a dirty habit.
Why do people drink?
That is a dirty habit.
You only flush it down the drain,
That is a dirty habit.
Why do people swear?
That is a dirty habit.
So why do people swear,
Oh what a dirty habit.

P L Kerr

Notes

Since September 1995 I have
had twenty poems published,
one of which was with the
International Society of Poets,
where I won The Editor's
Award for Outstanding
Achievement. I have had only
three rejections.

There is a good chance a
book of my own poetry will
be released sometime this
year, also I have enough poems for another book.

My first play, *The Torment of
Antonious,* is being considered for production and I am
now writing the sequel, *The
Power of the Ring.*

Although 1997 looks like it's
going to be a good year for
me, it also brings great sorrow, for I lost my father at
Christmas. He will be sadly
missed by myself, family,
relatives and friends.

Untitled

I sit in an empty room
        listening to everybody talking
Even though I'm on my own
        it's even more puzzling
I can't get a word in
        however hard I try
Sometimes I wonder
        should I give a heavy sigh
I light a cigarette
        and bang my head on the wall
Nobody even noticed
        when I fell on the floor
But enough is enough
        that I walked out the door
Then I remembered
        I have been here before

Anton Steffen

There's a Stranger

Notes

Jo was born in Harold Wood in Essex, and spent most of her life there until she married Edmund, in 1972. They now live in the village of Oakley, in Hampshire. They have a son, a married daughter and one grandchild.

Her interests include reading and writing and she has been writing poetry since her schooldays.

There's a stranger riding into town
He has a face of stone
All the folk have rushed inside
And left me on my own

This one is sure a killer
Mighty handy with a gun
But think nothin' of it
To shoot at anyone

There's a 'Wanted' poster out right now
Outside my office and jail
I've waited a mighty long time
For he shot my greatest pal

He sure is a hard mean man
With eyes of icy blue
With his hand poised on his gun
He's gonna try and kill me too

As he comes towards me
My hand shakes just a bit
No one else could chill my blood
As much as the Riley Kid

As his eyes bore into mine
I count from number one
And as I'm Sheriff of this town
Mighty quicker with my gun.

Jo Updale

My Four Year Old Niece

Notes

I am a mother of two boys. One is at college; the other graduated this year, 1996, from the University of Wales. One of my secret ambitions is to learn to play either the saxophone or the clarinet but no step has been taken for it to come to fruition.

Poetry had been part of my early school life and the recital of them. Every term at least one had to be learned and expressed with understanding. I do enjoy reading poetry but it's lately I realised I can create my own.

I would try an eraser but that wouldn't
do, to remove the mark
You left on my heart.
I have another thought
That nothing can be bought
To remove this dot
From this special spot.
So I decide to let it stay
The rubber I'll throw away
Because that's where a mark like that
belongs
On the heart, my dearest Breanne.

Vivienne Koo

Notes

I am a 65 going on 66 grandmother, living in Weston Super Mare with my husband. I have two lovely grandsons, Stuart (18) and Andrew (14). Stuart sometimes does my poems on his computer when I feel lazy.

I have only recently plucked up the courage to send any of my poems to be published, as I never thought they were any good. I write many of my poems when I am very happy or very sad. If you read my poem, *Life,* you will see it was a sad time. I have written about 150 poems, sometimes putting one in a birthday card or Christmas card.

My hobbies are writing poetry, walking my dog, bingo and doing crosswords.

Life

Life is full of happiness and sadness,
wildness, calm and even madness.
It's full of storms and winds,
and many immoral sins.
It's full of men and women that,
cheat and lie,
and will be the same until they die.
It's full of people ignorant and vain,
who enjoy giving others pain.
But as my spirit's very low,
I hope it's not really so. I pray out there
is love, happiness and fun,
enough for everyone.
And this dim view of mine,
will disappear in time.
And I will see a rosy glow,
in things and people that I know.

My wish for the future.

R I Jones

What is a Gran?

Notes

I am Jean Hendrie a 67 year old war widow and retired secretary. I have one son, Ian, (45 years old), four grand-sons, one granddaughter, two great-grandsons and one great-granddaughter.

I have six poems on tape (including three for the blind), seven editor's choice certificates for outstanding achievement in poetry for 1996, from the International Poets (London) and National Library of Poets (USA). *My Life and Thoughts in Verse.*

My hobbies include: writing poetry, family tree, oil-painting, singing, collecting stamps, coins and local post-cards.

I have written poetry for years but have only recently started to write seriously after the death of my only daugh-ter, Sheila. She died of cancer in June, 1995, aged 45 years. Also my husband John, who was wounded on D-Day, died in September, 1990, after suffering from war wounds and six heart attacks.

My first poem was published in Poetry Now in August, 1995. Since then I have written 126 poems, and so far have had 94 poems pub-lished in poetry books, magazines and in the local papers.

My inspiration comes from things that happen, my fam-ily, childhood days, past memories, my dog, my life and thoughts.

I found writing poetry was good therapy for me to over-come the grief of losing my husband and only daughter within five years.

A Gran, is a person,
　　Who will babysit, for free,
And tell the grand-kids stories,
　　As they sit, upon her knee.

She always sends them birthday cards,
　　And Christmas presents too,
Some folk, don't remember them,
　　But Grannies, always do.

But when the children, grow up,
　　Visiting Gran, becomes a bore,
Except, when asking favours,
　　Gran's not needed, anymore.

But when her life, is over,
　　They'll all begin, to cry,
'I used to love my Gran, so much,
　　Why did, she have to die.'

So they should try, to visit Grannie more,
　　In her advancing years,
And not wait, until her funeral,
　　To shed, their 'crocodile tears.'

Jean Hendrie

Notes

I am a lady of 71 years of age. I have a family of nine children, five boys and four girls, and twenty grandchildren. I was brought up in the East End of London, mostly the Stratford area, and I have recently moved to Rainham.

I have been writing poetry from the age of 10 years, but had never had any published until a short while ago: *The Mighty Sea* in Voices in the Wind, *Crabbed Age and Youth* in Jewels of the Imagination and now, *Moving House*. You can see what prompted that. I also knit and do crossword puzzles.

A Day in My Life

I get up at dawn, to start a new morn
Determined to be witty and bright
Within hours of three a totally new me
Has emerged with the coming of light
I cuss and I rave as I battle and slave
Over bed-making, washing and ironing.
The efforts worthwhile
'Cos I know I will smile
When everything's spotless and shining.
Alas and alack, I take it all back
As I hear the sounds of a car
The family comes in, pandemonium sets in
They have travelled from near and afar
It's so lovely to see them, but oh what a pain
I have to start all over again.

Josephine Madlin

Notes

I am Violet Mary Swaine, born in Suffolk in 1921, married without children. I am a retired police officer at present living in a retirement flat in King's Lynn, Norfolk.

My first interest in poetry was in 1930, when at the age of 9 years I was a member of the Children's Corner Club of the local newspaper, the Lowestoft Journal. A poetry competition was set and I entered this, with a poem entitled *God's Songsters* which won first prize.

Since then I have written odd verses in birthday cards and to friends. I wrote *Easter Thoughts* in 1993 for the Easter magazine for the Methodist Church of which I am a member. My present interests are helping with church events and in particular the Women's Fellowship.

Poetry seems to present itself to me whilst performing household chores, and only takes a short time to compile.

You Lucky People was sent to a friend with congratulations on a large lottery win.

You Lucky People

Was it five of the best and the Bonus,
    That made your lucky day,
I was thrilled when I heard about it,
    So congratulations I must say,
Had I been able to list winners,
    Your name would have been one come in view,
For it certainly couldn't have happened,
    To a nicer couple than you,
So enjoy an early retirement,
    And do those things you've most wanted to do,
And good health and good luck for the future,
    Is my final wish for you.

V Swaine

It's Up to Us

Notes

I am a forty-three year old single parent. I am the mother of two girls, Victoria and Jasmine, who are in their twenties and two boys, Ryan and Curtis who are in their teens.

I worry about my children's futures, I have seen what the effect of drugs have done to people in the past, how their personality completely changes and also how some become mentally unstable. A friend of mine hanged himself through taking drugs - it is something I will never get over.

I would like to dedicate this poem to him, my four children and to my dad, who passed away recently. I had a poem published recently, It's Up to Us is my second poem to be published. I only wish that my dad could have been here today to read them both.

The years are rolling quickly by.
The state of our world, it makes me cry.
The ozone layer, it's getting so thin.
The way we treat it is such a sin.
Do we not care about our future lot.
They are gonna suffer, it will be too hot.
In all our towns the smoke and fumes.
Will send our fore-kids to their dooms.
Are we not bothered, do we not care.
Is it because, we won't be there.
The ice is melting in our North Pole.
Our ozone layer has a gaping hole.
We feel no guilt and no remorse.
We have interfered with nature's course.
When we drive our cars, are we aware.
Of what's going on, do we really care.
There's so much danger for our kids to meet.
Like the fatal drugs that's on the street.
We must stop the pusher selling his gear.
To our innocent children we love so dear.
It's time for us to face the truth.
It's time to act and help our youth.
It's up to us our children's fate.
Come on let's act, we're not too late.
Do we not care, have we no shame.
When the earth goes pop, we are all to blame.

Imelda Bigley

In Memory of Mandy Frances

Notes

I am 53 years old and live in
Blidworth, Nottinghamshire
and work as a care-assistant
in a nursing home for the
elderly.

I started writing poetry about
eight years ago and have
luckily had nine poems published.

This poem is about my
daughter Mandy, who died in
1982 at the age of twenty.

*The poem is dedicated to her
and to all mothers who have
lost a precious child.*

With each waking thought I find,
Yet again you're on my mind.
Everywhere I go you're there,
Your presence lingers in the air.
In the flowers, in the trees,
I feel you on the passing breeze.
Everything I see and do,
Revives sweet memories of you.
In summer sun, in winter snow,
You walk beside me wherever I go.
In my heart and mind you'll always be,
Till the end of all eternity.

Avril Houlton

Sweet Treat

A cherry tree in the park
takes my notice.
Ah, such delicious red cherries
ripe to eat.
My hands reach up
I manage to get just one
The branches are far above me
I place the one cherry on my tongue
Sweet and juicy
I relish a treat.

Juliette Whitman

Nutty Me and My Saucy Crockery

Notes

Recently I had a poem published in the delightful anthology Rhyme and Reason, entitled *Noah's Ark*.

While in the stages of the making of this book my tutor whom I have speech lessons with told me to broaden my horizons. My next adventure, a pantomime I wrote for North Warwickshire College, Nuneaton, I am pleased to say will be performed by the Youth Theatre at Christmas 1997.

I am already working on my next script, a science fiction spoof. When completed I hope to sell it to television.

For Day by Day I contribute a delicious poem entitled, Nutty Me and my Saucy Crockery, inspired by the poetry of Spike Milligan.

So it is only appropriate to dedicate this poem to my tutor, Pam Weston, and a favourite of mine, Spike Milligan.

The sun was sunny, birds sung spellbound unto beauty, the sky was blue.
Scenery was green, pity I was heading toward Funny Farm
honestly you haven't a clue.

I could not get out of my head a dish having an affair with the spoon.
Why? Well the spoon had been seeing the mug
but the mug was in love with the jug.
The jug fancied the knife, for good or for life
and the knife preferred the plate.
The plate was friendly with the saucer,
the saucer had a crush on the teapot
and the teapot, well the teapot was into prostitution.
And that's why the dish ran away with the spoon.

The men in white suits don't believe these stories.
They laugh and they joke, say I'm full of Jackanory.
They wind me up, say do I fancy a cup
typical humorous Tories.

Jim Buckingham

261

Notes

There seems no finality about divorce - little comfort as in death. Just speculation on who got it wrong. It affects the whole family so much like wearing armbands without tears.

This has happened to both myself and my daughter. I wrote this poem for her and her daughters.

Poem for Jane

What is this life so full of thugs
Endless drink and damaging drugs
Another murder,
Another child,
A Grandma's body just recovered
Who did it?
Will they ever discover?

What's in this world
There seems so much
Designer clothes
And endless money
But nothing fits
Nothing's funny,
Tears, tragedies,
Lives torn apart
Too many tears
And broken hearts.

M Phillips

The Garden

Notes

I am 63 years old and live in sheltered housing, in Blackley, Manchester. I have five sons and eight grandchildren.

I started writing about eighteen months ago. As my days were occupied caring for my husband, Stanley, I found that writing was something I could do and still be 'there' for him.

I have also written several short stories for children but have never attempted to have any of my work published, until now. I have always done it for Stanley and my grandchildren and I hope that it has given them as much pleasure as I have had writing them.

When Stanley was fit he spent every spare moment he had in his garden and it was quite usual for him to be out at 5 am to get in a couple of hours before his working day, running his own small coach business, began.

As his health became worse and he was unable to walk he got round his garden on his electric scooter. Eventually his eyesight went and he could no longer manage to do it. When we moved into sheltered housing in 1994 I had to become his eyes and legs. I have been alone since July 1996.

I would like to dedicate this poem, together with all the others I have written about him, to Stanley with my love. Without his help, encouragement and interest they might never have been written. Thank you.

Stan's garden was at Cheltenham Road
He made it right from scratch
He dug the soil, he built the walls
So they would always match.

He laid the grass so green and fresh
He made the paths as well
He made the pond, the fountain too
It really did look swell.

He planted flowers, he planted trees
He planted bushes too.
Tomatoes and some grapes he had
He watched them as they grew.

The fish he had lived in the pond
The frogs lived in there too
He planted water lilies there
And watched the fish swim through.

Daffs in the front garden, Daffs in the back
Tulips on the patio, Fuchsias hanging up
Apple trees and cherry trees laden down with fruit
Azalea, Lobelia where else can they be put

The day came when he had to leave
This garden filled with beauty
No longer could he see the flowers
What he loved became a duty.

Now here he is in Hudson Court
But he cannot walk or see
His friends have helped and done their best
Is this how it will always be?

Eileen Bradshaw

Notes

I hope when my time comes to depart this world, there is a better place to go to, and the people I have loved and lost will be there to welcome me.

A Better Place

What is out there in outer space?
Are there angels with wings of lace?
Is there a golden gate with a silver bell?
Is there a mansion where good people dwell?
Are there lights that never go out?
Are there cherubs with lips that pout?
Are there fields of emerald grasses?
Are there flowers growing in masses?
Is there in charge a wise old man?
Is there really an evil ban?
Are there my loved ones, lost and dear?
Are their loving arms waiting to hold me near?
If there is such a place above?
In peace I'll leave this life I love.

Sylvia Duncan

Growing Old

Notes

Born in Kensington, London, I now live in Basingstoke, Hampshire, with my parents. In my forties, single and working in a job where I meet people from all walks of life, gives me the opportunity to put pen to paper. What inspired me in the first place was when our local paper printed my first poem, called *Getting Old*.

I would like to say thanks to Poetry Today for selecting another of my works for their new book.

Trees of green,
skies of blue,
that we have seen,
I've got eyes for you.

When we met,
our love grew fonder,
a life was set,
as our lives went yonder.

As the years past,
our children grew,
middle-age upon fast,
soon we'll be looking for life anew.

Now we have seen,
that we are old,
but still see trees of green,
they of course have grown old.

Steve Wright

Notes

I was born in Dorset in a small village called Kingston. My father was the local carpenter/blacksmith as was his family before him for over 200 years. I live with my husband David, Ross our Doberman dog, and Quaver our cat. We live in a seaside town on the North Norfolk coast, where we have lived for 26 years.

My daughter Louise is married and lives in Tunisia, her husband works for British Gas. They have recently presented us with our first granddaughter, Abigail. Stuart our son is married and is a manager in a local accountant firm, his wife, Alison, is a nurse.

My family are very important to me and we are all good friends taking pleasure and interest in each others company. My hobbies are reading, walking, swimming, writing letters and singing.

I worked as a community nurse in the district caring for the sick and elderly for 15 years until I retired in 1995. I now work casually for a residential home for the elderly.

I was inspired to write *The Highlands* from memories also family connections in Scotland.

I would like to thank my family for encouragement and support in the writing of my poetry.

The Highlands

Over the mountains
Down in the glens.
Deer are grazing
Hiding from men.

The moors are so mystic
As the stream runs past.
With a Loch in the distance
Where fishermen cast.

Heathers are blooming
Across the moors.
Where grouse are roaming
Along the shores.

Salmon leap in rivers deep
The waters are so clear.
Highland cows with shaggy coats
Stand by a castle near.

Sheep graze on the hillside
In their woolly coats.
Waterfalls are running
As ducks fly by in groups.

The eagle flies high in the sky
It really is a sight.
Suddenly it swooped and dived
Its colours clear and bright.

Puffins roosting on the cliffs
The ferry-boats go by.
Seals are basking in the sun
Whilst geese are flying high.

Mountains in the background
An owl hoots in the night.
The day is now drawing nigh
As the stars shine in the sky.

Aves Swanson

One Street Boy

Notes

I am married to Alf, I have one son David, a daughter-in-law Lynne, a granddaughter Nina and a grandson Jack. My family are situated down in the Midlands, so as I live near Blackpool, I see them only on special occasions, but I am provided with a progress report by phone every week, so it's not too bad.

I am a Christian and also a Humanitarian, I have many friends both in my Christian circles and in other walks of life. I care greatly about other people's welfare also the plight of our animal kingdom, that's why I choose to be a vegetarian.

I feel that our way of life at this present time does not show the slightest interest in what is happening in our society today when I wrote One Street Boy, I tried hard to put myself into this young lad's life. I can honestly say it is not easy, I come to realise that we just can't comprehend the trauma some of these children have been put through and unless we were put into the same situation we could never even come close to understanding, but there is a way out, if anyone is prepared to take it, and that is by putting your faith and trust in a man called Christ Jesus. He is the only way to take the heartache and the pain away, and he does give new life for old, he can and does provide. Don't take my word for it, try him for yourself.

As I walked the streets alone
No food, no clothes, no home
I paused and looked around me
As people passed me by
No one caring if I should live or die
As my thoughts flashed back on my life
I remember my days as a child
No comfort, no joy, no love could I see
Only bruises and screaming and hell there for me
As I carried on walking the streets that night
Looking for shelter from the winds that bite
What I was thinking of my early days
Was the humiliation and grieve my parents gave
My fears turned into nightmares
Walking the streets that night
Looking for a bed to rest my head
Knowing it'll be a cardboard box instead

People stopped and stared that night
I was on my own with nothing but fright
Then I looked up at the heavens above
And said, 'Please Lord Jesus, send me your love'
Then I heard a voice saying, 'Lean on me
Take my hand and walk with me
We'll spend this night together you and me
And I'll be a friend to you,' said he,
Now I've a saviour, I have found
Who'll keep me warm, and safe and sound
He'll stay with me all through the night
And he'll be there by the morning light
Now I was lost but now I'm found
For my God's love will always be around
And I feel sorry for the folks who stared
Maybe some day they too, will hear his word
My life is happy now all the day
With my Lord around come what may
He will help me, and he'll always stay
For now I'm his, and he is mine
This Lord this Saviour of mankind.

J Murray

The Arrival

Notes

I am 53 years old, I have five children, all grown now, and seven grandchildren. I have not had time to write until now, but I love writing poetry and songs - I am inspired by everyday events.

My ambition is to have a children's story published. Candy, one of my daughters is a talented artist and I should like her to illustrate my story book.

I dedicate this poem to my grandson, Levi, in celebration of the birth of his sister Josephine.

It started at three in the morning
The worry, was everything right
Is it really beginning to happen
Or just a bad dream in the night

No, I'm sure I'm awake now, not dreaming
And I'd better go check on the rest
Get Joe packing the car
And young Levi is up
Now I can get myself dressed

I can hardly believe I'm excited
But yes, I am really quite pleased
Did I pack everything that I needed?
And the kitchen sink too, Joe teased
'Go ring up my sister Candy'
I knew it was time to report
'Get the whole family out here'
I said, as I gripped my support

A series of lip-biting spasms
And I thought that the end was quite near
Then the very last pain, the trip was not in vain
The very beautiful Josephine is here.

Candy Sampson

Passing the Buck

Notes

I first discovered poetry at the age of twelve, when a piece I wrote as part of a school project was selected as the best in my year. All of the winning pupils had to read their poem out in front of the school, during the morning assembly. I can remember being absolutely terrified, but at the same time, strangely intrigued by the excitement my poetry had generated. It was this experience that inspired me to take up poetry as a full-time hobby.

I stopped writing when I left home at the age of sixteen and didn't write again until four years later, when I split up with a girlfriend. I found by writing my problems down in the form of a poem, I was better able to come to terms with them. I also found the task remarkably easy.

Since that day, I haven't looked back and now write more confidently than ever before. Unlike many other poets, I have no ambitions of becoming the next Shakespeare or Wordsworth; I want to be the new Marvyn B Candler with my own unique style and interpretations. It is my belief that through my poetry I am able to help people get in touch with their true feelings.

So I've done it once or twice,
What's wrong with that?
Compared to him next door
I'm not that bad.
Now wait a minute,
Don't exaggerate!
A bloke at work
Does it every day.
And what about her
At number sixty three,
She's always at it,
She's much worse than me.
A friend of mine
Does it five times a night,
And what about Harry,
He does it in daylight.
Talk about me,
What about you?
You do it
Much more that I do.
So I do it quite often,
There's nothing wrong with that,
Compared to everyone else
I'm not that bad.

Marvyn B Candler

Abandoned in Surrey

Notes

I started writing poetry in
1995 and have had several
poems published in anthologies and magazines.

Aside from poetry, my hobbies include gardening, particularly herb growing and
wine-making. I also belong to
the University of the Third
Age.

Since retiring, I have enjoyed
travelling abroad.

I've been here a week, abandoned, alone
Ignored by most folks passing by
Sometimes I'm moved to another zone
Will someone please tell me why?

I ponder what will become of me
I feel out of place, in the way
The man who left me perhaps thought he
Would be better without me that day

I hate the cold and the dark winter nights
When it rains I get soaked to the core
Too miserable even to enjoy passing sights
I just want to return to my store

If you see me won't you please take me home
At work I love life and I'm jolly
My owners prefer it when I do not roam
So pray return this poor superstore trolley.

Yvonne V Smith

Caravaning in Scotland

Notes

I was born in Liverpool 1926, married to John and have three children, Paul, Angela and Brian. I also have three grandchildren, Emily, Emma and Oliver.

I started painting landscapes and writing poetry after my retirement.

We lived in Scotland for twenty years and loved the country and its warm and friendly people.

It was after a caravan holiday in the Highlands that I wrote this poem about *Caravaning in Scotland.*

Mobile homes, nameless faces
Settling down in various places
Happy children content and free
Roam the pastures, swim in the sea.

Fairyland castles, gardens of flowers
Childhood picnics to while away the hours
Distillers to visit, whiskey to taste
Heather's to purchase, salmon to grace

The visitors table, the anglers line
As we quietly savour the passage of time
The whirl of the tartan, the sound of the pipes
Scenes to remember and cherish for life.

Mary

Notes

I am 43 years old and have seven brothers and three sisters. We were all raised in a little village in East Sussex called Buxted which is where I now live. My parents names are Joyce and Clarence Blackford. I have three children, Terry (24), Mitch (22) and Cecilia (16). I also have a grandson, Kelvin, he is five years old.

Having my grandson to stay every third weekend is very special to me. In my spare time I enjoy decorating, gardening and playing stoolball.

I have only been writing poetry for the last one and a half years. So far Poetry Today have published one of my other poems, entitled, *Special Pen-friend* in their book Rhyme and Reason.

I wrote this poem, *The Heartaches of Drugs* about my son, Terry. He is now living with me and is off drugs but is still waiting to go into a Rehabilitation Centre.

The Heartaches of Drugs

My son was just any ordinary child,
But he grew up to be very wild.
His teenage years were spent at raves,
He became so aggressive during them days.
Later he went on to doing *E's*,
No matter how I tried I could not please,
This teenager was getting out of hand,
But I Just felt I could not stand,
Around and put up with his moody ways,
It had been going on for days and days,
So his bags were packed and off he went,
A few months later a message I was sent,
A girlfriend he was living with was having his baby,
I thought then perhaps he would maybe,
Sort his life out once and for all,
Oh I must have been such a fool,
Because after the baby's presence was felt,
All my son done was to gauche out,
He started to experiment with speed,
But to nothing but trouble did that lead.
The police were always at his place,
Sometimes I didn't know were to put my face,
A move of house was on the cards,
And I know for the baby's sake he tried very hard,
But drugs messed his life up,
He was just in one big rut.
The next thing I knew he was doing smack,
I knew this time there was no turning back,
A heroine addict he has become,
And I myself know what this has done,
Ruined his life, that's for sure.
His girlfriend kicked him out the door,
In a hotel he now resides,
But most of the time he just hides,
Away from life and all it holds,
What drugs have done to him please be told,
A rehabilitation centre is were he is waiting to go,
But although I've tried no one wants to know,
So every night when I go to bed,
I pray that up to heaven he will not be lead.

Angela Hazelden

Notes

I am a 75 year old man. I have written poetry since 1938. Although I have been told, from time to time, that I should be published, I have not thought my work good enough.

I love walking, visiting gardens and parks, and meeting people.

I write mostly about what I see and people I meet.

Life's Mystery

Life is full of mystery
Look around and you will find
Things that need explaining
Things to test your mind.

How is it an animal walks
As soon as it is born
Why do weeds always bloom
In a gardeners lawn.

The bad weather is over
At the end of May
So why does it start to rain
On a summer holiday.

But the biggest mystery
The one that beats them all
Is how your drinking pal is missing
When it's his turn to call.

Or when the fags are handed round
You take turns about
When it comes to his turn
He has just run out.

R T Illingworth

That Darned Cat

Notes

That Darned Cat, is dedicated to a naughty little cat called Billy. Yes, Billy the cat, wherever you are now!

That darned cat, rushed across the room.
I tripped on the mat and then went zoom.
Collided with the chair, then I lost my hair.
My wig came off and landed on the mat,
And some how finished up on the head of the cat.

He strolled around, he looked such a scream,
He went into the kitchen,
And he ate a bowl of cream.
He walked down the street, swishing his tail,
And stopped off at the pub
For a pint of ale.

He got quite drunk and rolled on the mat.
The punters said 'What's wrong with that cat?'
The cat lay down, to sleep it off,
Then walked down the street,
Looking like a toff.

He got back home, after his *roam*,
Round his mouth was a layer of foam.
He licked off the foam, the remainder of the ale,
He walked down the garden,
Looking hearty and hale.

A breeze came up, and blew round the shed,
And took the wig right off his head.
The wig went up and landed in a tree,
And no one knew what it could be.
A passer-by said 'Mercy me,
There's a cat stuck in a tree!'

He rushed and called the fire brigade,
With a rescue ladder for his aid.
The man went up, with a helmet on his head,
And said 'Cor blimey, I think he's dead!'

He gave the *body* a fireman's lift,
And backed down the ladder, before it could shift.
He got down the bottom, the *body* not stirred,
And for a moment, no one said a word.

Then, all of a sudden, the cat strolled by,
With a glint in his eye.
He picked up the wig and tossed it on his head,
For after all, it was really dead.
He strolled around, he looked such a scream,
He went into the kitchen and he ate a bowl of cream.

Jane Owen

My Window

From my window
What can I see?
I can see the sea
Boats drift by
Gulls do fly
Friends pass by
Call in for tea,
The lawn is green
More to be seen
Flowers all hues
Red, pink and blues
Sky at night
Stars all bright
There's the moon
Morning soon!

J M Taylor

Peace in Argyll

Notes

I am a Scottish water colour artist who is inspired in poetry and art by the beauty of my country. I live partly in Argyll and partly in Suffolk, but hope to return to Scotland permanently. Most of my twelve grandchildren live in Suffolk and Norfolk, so that is why I am partly in the south. They also write poetry and paint, as do my own five children. My husband has died.

As a child I had long carefree holidays with my family. We made our own entertainment with boats and bicycles, sailing, climbing and fishing. My late husband and I carried on this tradition with our children.

I have an award from The International Library of Poetry and have had poems in Poetry Today. Other poems have been published in The Scots Magazine, Scottish Poets, Simple Pleasures Poetry Book and Rhyme Arrival. My paintings are in various exhibitions.

Bracken and rushes and birches
Golden and rust and brown,
Shells on the shore,
Birds in the bay,
Who could want more?
Beauty all day.
Night with the stars on the dark loch,
Night with the wind in the tree,
Hills and rocks in the moonlight,
Here you are wild and free.
Brown running burn in the heather,
Sun dew, and moss on the stone,
Wild as the eagle above you,
Here you are always alone.
Mist and the clouds on a boulder,
Otter and fish in the bay,
Deer on the hill,
Trees by the shore,
Beauty all round,
Who would want more!

June Cooke

Slimming

I'm a large lady, full and round
All to easy to put on the pounds,
I diet and diet until I feel faint
Oh, to be slim and to look quite quaint.

Lettuces so green, tomatoes so red
Get slim, get slim, words going through My head.
Don't fry this, but you must always grill
What on earth can this stomach of mine fill.

I'm willing to try this and also that
I'm fighting the bulge and still I'm fat,
I've even tried the slimming pill
But all it did was make me feel ill.

I hope one of these days to be slim
With a nice figure, neat and trim,
With nice clothes and a nice dress
Will I feel better? Is anyone's guess.

Mavis Shaw

Our Cats

Notes

I am 58 years old and have been married to John for 34 years. We have two grown up daughters, one son, and three grandchildren, Simon, Robert and Emily.

I was born in Hitchin, Hertfordshire and have lived in Sandy for 26 years.

I have always enjoyed writing poetry. *The Gossip* is due to be published in Awaken to a Dream and *Sunday* has been published in Rhyme and Reason.

They hunt all night and sleep all day
In their lazy cat-like way.
Curled up, snoozing in a ball
Until they hear the night owl call.

No bird is safe within its nest
No mouse may linger for a rest,
No bat, or rat, or vole or mole
Is happy in its hidden hole.

No fish, or newt, or frog or toad
Is safe within its own abode
And even things like little deer
Have been known to disappear!

The heron is a graceful bird
And very seldom seen or heard.
Who'd think that one as large as that
Would fall a victim of the cat!

And when the night is all but done
And both the cats have had their fun,
They come back home and purr and play
Then sleep again all through the day.

Janet Jones

Notes

I live in the picturesque village of Blisworth in Northamptonshire. I have two adult children, named Stuart Anthony and Melanie-Jayne. I was widowed this year, 1996. I wrote a poem, regarding widowhood, which is to be published in a magazine at a later date. Hopefully, this poem will comfort the hearts of other widows, as they, with me, walk the difficult path of bereavement.

I inherited the great gift of poetry from my mother, who's still having poetry published at the age of 79. I began writing in 1986, but didn't submit my work until the autumn of 1993. The first poem submitted - *A Season of Mists* - was published at this time. It was inspired, of course, by the colours and mists of this glorious season, which happens to be my favourite.

I write prose, and also poetry, on religion, hilarious odes and anything that stimulates a vivid imagination. Since 1993, I've had forty seven poems published; there are others awaiting consideration. This year, 1996, I received three Editor's Choice awards: one poem is to be presented on tape, accompanied by commentary with a background of baroque music.

Words are my world; I hope you enjoy my poem, *Misty Magic.*

These words are for you - the bereaved: I reach out to you - as others have, to me, in my loss. The power, of the written word, was made known to me, through the feedback from others, in response to the verses that I wrote for them in their time of grief.

The Bliss of Solitude

When hearts break and sorrow cleaves,
    there's no happy interlude.
But one day, in the mists of time,
there'll be the bliss of solitude.

There is no easy way, through loss -
    there's no escaping pain;
But bliss, is never out of reach,
when faith can ease the strain.

Hold nothing back - let teardrops fall,
    to release that ache inside.
'Cos there'll be no blissful moments,
until you've cried - and cried.

The peace you need is kept at bay,
    'til the process is complete:
    For grief can bring enrichment,
    a phase that's bitter-sweet.

Just bear in mind - I've been there too:
I'm no stranger, to the ways of grief,
and I've felt the way, you're feeling now:
    it's almost beyond belief!

But one day, in the mists of time,
    there'll be a change of mood;
when at last, you have a well
earned share, in the bliss, of solitude.

Patricia Mary Gross

Notes

I am Jacqueline Bentley, 49 years old, married to John and have two sons, Stephen and Andrew. I own and run a village shop in Pirbright, Surrey.

My hobbies include nature, and I spend a great deal of time walking in the countryside. I have also done a lot of walking on the Lleyn Peninsula.

This is my tenth poem to be published and my inspiration comes from writing about things of beauty.

The Wye Valley is just a suitable distance from where I live to go away for a quiet weekend. The hotel mentioned is very tranquil and I wrote this poem whilst staying there. The walks along the river are beautiful and the air is fresh, giving one a sense of well-being.

Ice-Cream

The little boy went into the shop,
He was such a little dot.
The sweets were high and he couldn't see,
So he asked a chap to hold him up on his knee
He saw what he wanted and made a grab,
The sweets toppled over with an almighty crash.

The boy started crying,
The owner started shouting
What happened to my sweets,
The man holding him started laughing
Then they decided to have a party.

They flicked ice-cream on the walls and doors,
Black and white, red and green,
A disgusting mess that couldn't be cleaned.
The little boy awoke from his dream
His mother asked him if he would like ice-cream.

Jacqueline Bentley

Hope

Notes

I am a widow with three school-age children.

I was first introduced to poetry at 14, when one lesson per week was dedicated to the writing of such. I gained much pleasure in completing them. Through my adolescence, I suffered very much from insecurity. I thought, once married, my life would become less confused and purposeful.

The birth of my first son brought great joy but also fear. At the age of 6 to 8 weeks, medical staff were uncertain if he would survive. Against the odds, he fought back and achieved what others thought impossible. He not only survived, but is now relatively healthy.

The birth of my twins was another great event, yet tinged with fear. The smallest, at only 2lbs 5oz at birth and 6lbs at 4½ months, underwent open-heart surgery at Great Ormond Street Hospital. It was during his convalescence that the strain became too much for me. During the next few weeks, whilst resting, I wrote a poem, called *Life*.

I have written several others, usually after traumatic experiences, including one entitled *Jerry*, which I completed recently on the death of my husband. I am working towards publication of a book.

When life has lost its sparkle and god seems far away
You wake to a brand new morning one bright and sunny day
and realise your quest in life is no impossible goal
but now is well within your grasp to make your existence whole.

Life gains another meaning not the void of yesterday
you suddenly find direction and steer another way
Towards a brighter future away from the murky past
that had you almost beaten until the very last.

That little ray of hope that once was never there
ignites that spark within your heart and suddenly you care
about the future that never was and now it is to be
The hope not only for yourself but all your family

You realise the hope you found can easily be lost
you must never be complacent or be it to your cost
The heavy burdens are no more your journey begins again
Your prayer finally answered for hope and life
Amen.

Nicola Martin

Autumn Years

Notes

I am Fred Norgrove born April 1911 in Bristol the youngest of five children. I was encouraged to read and write poetry at Dr Bell's C of E School, Fishponds, Bristol. I left school at 14 and spent my working life on building sites and as a factory machinist. I experienced the poverty of the 1920's.

I wrote a little in my youth but my first serious poem came late in life, entitled *Galloping Hooves*, police v miners 1984-85. I now write regularly as a member of a Christian Fellowship, Long Crendon Baptist Church, which are mostly monologues venturing down memory lane. A cassette tape recorded 1995 entitled *Autumn Years*. I have had two poems accepted for publication entitled *Thoughts in a Garden* and *A New Dawn*.

Gone are eighty five summers
If I remembered something from each and every one
I realise the disappointment looking back would bring
Remembering things I could and should have done
My boyhood and schooldays were happy
In my youth there were years quite sad
It was then I often questioned our Lord's will
Often envying what others had.
In my youth my mother taught me a lesson
It was the Lord's will that we had been born poor
We must accept and really cling to his promises
There was no doubt they would be kept, my mother was sure
The harder our cross on this earth my son
The brighter our crown in heaven will be
In life's journey through these eighty five years my mother's
                                        vision I too now can see.
Through our Lords grace I've had the blessings of a family
knowing the love a wife and children can bring
Our Lord has called my sweetheart and my son to His heavenly home
These words I can joyfully sing
Safe in the arms of Jesus, safe on his gentle breast
No more for them the trials of this world
They are sharing his love in peace and rest
I'll put behind me all the sadness and pain
I'll give thanks for the blessings I've had
Today I am very happy, tomorrow I won't be sad.
For tomorrow never comes, the dawn brings another to-day
So thank you Lord for these eighty five years
This is what I pray
Closer much closer to thee Lord, that is my goal toward the
                                        end of my days.
However much longer you grant me Lord
I will try and give you unending praise.

Fred Norgrove

Why?

Notes

I am 29 years old, married with two lovely little girls, Lisa, aged 6 and Helen, aged 4.

I cannot work as I am a severe epileptic, I have at least two seizures a day. I have suffered since I was ten years old. Earlier this year I underwent brain surgery for the epilepsy, unfortunately it hasn't worked.

I am a Roman Catholic and I enjoy going to church.

I was about 10 years old when I wrote my first poem. I have quite a good collection of them now on various subjects. I have had a couple published and one day I would like to have my own book.

Different things inspire my poems. My husband gives me topics, and also my own ideas of every day life gives me ideas of what to write about.

Why is a question always asked me
Such as why do we all have a family tree?
Why are our children so very quick?
Why do the clocks annoy me and tick?
Why does the bath water suddenly go cold?
Why do us youngsters eventually grow old?
Why does the morning come very soon?
Why can't we always have a full moon?
Why are some people fat, and some rather slim?
Why are some happy, and some rather grim?
Why does the summer go very fast?
Yet the winter takes a long time to go past
Why do footballer's have to be good with a ball?
Why do policemen have to be tall?
How is it that *why* is often heard?
But can often be an annoying word
So always remember when talking to mates
Never to bring *why* into debates.

Sally Elizabeth Burton

Notes

I began writing late in life when I started with children's short stories and poems for my three year old grandson. I then went on to write poems and some short stories for adults and so far have been quite successful in getting a few into print. It is an interesting hobby and my other main interest is ballroom dancing which I taught for many years but now it is just a social pastime.

I am married to Kenneth and have a daughter, Vanessa and a grandson, Mark.

I live in Cheltenham, not far from the racecourse and I was educated at the local Grammar School.

My poem *Dolly* was written in the early years when my grandson was 3 years old.

Dolly

Dolly was a beauty
With a nose so cute and small
But Dolly wasn't very nice
Not very good at all.

Dolly looked an angel
With eyes of brilliant blue
But Dolly was a naughty girl
Much worse than me - or you.

Dolly looked so pretty
Her hair a lovely gold
But Dolly would have tantrums
And shout and scream I'm told.

My mum thought I was naughty
Till Dolly came to stay
But now she thinks I'm very good
And praises me each day.

I'm glad dolly Came to stay.

Jeanette L Durk

Golden Windows

Notes

I was born Bridget Elizabeth Barker 19th December 1934 at Bilby, Worksop, Nottinghamshire. Father being a farm worker I enjoyed a country upbringing. Imagination needed for amusement. Being born with dislocated hips I spent long periods in hospital. I married and had five children. We then brought up our grandson Ricky for whom *Golden Windows* was written.

Poetry has been with me for as long as I can remember. I started to write them down with either morals or to amuse the children. I am interested in many things: dogs, having bred shih-tzu for ten years, plants and watercolour painting. The problem being to find enough hours to fit everything in. This year the International Library of Poetry are publishing two of my poems. and awarded me an Editor's Certificate of Merit. With five poems published it is so exciting. I have to thank my husband and my mother for encouraging me, Harry Eyre and Emily Barker.

We retired ten years ago to the lovely Nantle Valley Snowdonia and my husband is a retired nurse.

Golden windows shining bright
Guide my way to sleep to night
When I awake you will be gone
But your bright light still burns on.

May it guide you through the years
A light to aim for through the tears
When everything is wrong today
Golden windows not far away

Your going to learn a lost that's new
Only learn what shines out true
So when you're grown you can say
Golden windows lit my way

B Eyre

My Dad

Notes

My name is Noreen Kerrison and I am fifty years old, married with four children: three daughters and one son. I live in a small market town called Bungay, in Suffolk.

My family, religion and friends are important and very special to me in my life. My hobbies include: watercolour painting, Calligraphy, walking, gardening and of course writing poems.

My special interest at the moment is the biography I am writing about my Dad's life and experiences as a POW in the Second World War, held prisoner by the Germans.

I have had one other poem published called, *The Long Hot Summer.* I started writing poetry three years ago when my Dad died. I found it helped a great deal with my emotions, enabling me to cope with a great loss.

This poem was written, just after the first anniversary of my Dad's death, I miss him so much it seems almost as if some part of me is missing and can never be found!

This poem is dedicated to my dearest Dad. To the world he was one, to me he was the world. I love you Dad.

It's over a year now
since my Dad passed away,
I'm loving him, missing him
with each passing day,
It's not been at all easy
I often feel sad,
Angry, frustrated, and really quite mad
That he was taken away
while I was not there,
I was in your house Lord
Kneeling in prayer,
Oh! please dear Lord help me
help me to feel glad,
Glad that he's with you
in his heavenly home,
Freed from all suffering
freed from all pain,
Don't let me be selfish
and wish him back here,
Oh! Lord I can't help it
I want him to be near,
So I can tell him, I love him
tell him I care,
Please tell him for me Lord
Please answer my prayer . . .

Noreen Kerrison

Notes

I am 57 years old and live with my 88 year old mother in Littledale Pickering, although I am originally from London. I worked for Lyon's Maid for 28 years but have now retired.

I have not, as yet, had any of my own work published.

My hobbies are photography, and writing, which I started about three months ago when I joined a WEA class in Scarborough.

My inspiration is from ideas that just come to me and my interest in the sea.

For a Summers Day

Far away upon a cloud
up down dale
Pretty flowers dance in the wind
So slowly blowing to and fro
To and fro in the wind
colours red, pink, blue, yellow
Still the show
On the wind a kite will blow
dancing gladly as if unleashed
a free thing adrift
as if alive to wonder at will
Above the tree tops high
Unaided on the breeze,
The moon looks down
Smiling at the scene
as it gathers speed again.
along the way
a drop of rain in the air.
The flowers appear joyful
of the rain
They feel rejuvenated
Spring to life anew
Over house tops fly
The kite so high
Wishing to rest awhile
along the way
Until it meets a tree top high
and rests gently down
on its branches wide
resting, sighing, unable
to untangle itself
from its branches
Staying fixed until the wind
sets it free again to fly
on but the kite feels weary
a tear appears and down it comes
upon the ground so damp
no more to fly high
The kite no more to move.

Jane Minter

My School Days

Notes

I became widowed when I was 38 years of age and my husband was 39. I was left with three sons - twins of 18 years old who were called up for National Service three months later - and one at school, 13 years of age. My widow's pension was cut down to ten shillings a week when he became 14. I took a job to make ends meet.

My youngest son was killed in an accident at the age of 35, leaving two children whom I helped to rear. I'm now 82 years of age; I've been housebound for ten years, suffering with osteoarthritis, a heart condition and a cancerous tumour. I'm not very active but I manage to knit, do tapestry and write, even though in constant pain.

I have a poem being published by The International Library of Poetry, entitled *Autumn Leaves*, and another being published by Anchor Books. I first began writing poetry as a pastime, eight years ago. Memories of loved ones lost gave me inspiration - they are connected with any personal feelings.

Inspiration to write *Torture of Grief* came to me on the memoriam date of my husband's death - I felt so sad and alone. I relived all the trauma of his long-suffering illness - all the plans we had made - my thoughts raced on and on.

My inspiration occurs spontaneously and covers a variety of things, mostly ones connected with my own personal life.

When I was a child at school
We were taught the golden rules,
To be obedient and polite,
Not to quarrel or to fight
To learn to spell, read and write
and to do our homework every night,
To sit upright and not to slouch
Lest we would grow a nasty hump
no crouching over lesson books
always neat and tidy look,
Hair well back from off our face
Ribbon or slide to keep it in place
To respect our teacher and others too
To take pride in all we do,
Children in those far off days,
Differed much in many ways
Compared to many of today,
Who always want to have their way,
and if they don't - it's sad to say
They make our lives a hellish day.

O M Godfrey

Things are Changing

Notes

Born at Pilsley on the Chatsworth estate in 1934, where my father was baker and post-master.

We moved to Leicestershire when I was 18 months old to take over the family baking and confectionery business at Houghton-on-the-Hill.

My father was a Methodist local preacher, my mother also spoke at ladies meetings. As a child I spent many hours listening to my mother recite poetry.

When my father remarried after the death of my mother, I moved to West Bridgford where I now teach organ and piano.

I have been writing poetry for about 10 years, the inspiration for *Things are Changing*, came one spring, trying on summer dresses and finding some were too small.

I'm sure my bath towel's shrinking, it doesn't cover me anymore.
And my clothes are getting smaller, behind my wardrobe door.
I must have grown an inch this year cause it's further to the floor.
And the hill is getting steeper, they've moved that bus stop, I am sure.

The news paper print is smaller, I noticed it today.
And the volume on my TV set is fading, I would say.
People don't speak clearly now, it fills me with dismay.
Is this just an awful dream? Please let it go away.

Even though I'm growing older I really can't complain.
I've had a life of love and joy and mostly free from pain.
Though the younger world around me is going quite insane.
If I had the chance to start afresh, I'd do it all again.

We see the world is dancing now to the beat of a different drum.
A great man said that youth was wasted on the very young.
But we do waste our later years, the time that is to come.
Help me to live my life today, to walk if I cannot run.

Rosemary Garfoot

Notes

I am 20 years old from a small town called Ollerton in Nottinghamshire.

Much of my time is devoted to my religious beliefs, but in my spare time I find writing poetry very relaxing and it gives me an opportunity to write down my deepest thoughts and feelings. It is a relief to be able to express such things in writing rather than keep them all bottled up inside. I also enjoy watching and participating in many kinds of sporting activities.

I Have It All is one of my favourite poems. It reminds me of all that I have to be thankful for.

I would like to dedicate this poem to my family and friends who help me appreciate that you do not have to be materially wealthy to be rich.

I Have It All

Sometimes I wish I were alone
Just to see how it would be
In an empty field on my own
Or on a boat out at sea
But then I stop to think a while
About the kind of life I lead
And then I find I start to smile
I know I have all I need
I have my friends and family
I have my God in whom I trust
I have the truth which sets me free
Do I have it all? I think I must.

C Hesford

Notes

I am a widow aged 76 and have three children and six grandchildren. I live in Taunton, Somerset.

This is the first time I have been published commercially. I have never gained a prize or award from my writing. I am a member of Taunton Branch of the University of the Third Age, and convenor of the Creative Writing Group.

My hobbies are photography and reading.

I have written poetry, on and off, since I was at school and have been writing seriously for about ten years.

Inspiration comes to me suddenly, from something I hear, or see on television, something I experience or 'just out of the blue'.

This poem is dedicated to my granddaughter who was my inspiration for the poem.

Memories

An empty beach,
An evening sun
Shining on a stooping child
Peering in a rock pool.

Images that haunt my mind
Through years that come and go,
Where now that quiet beach
And child, absorbed?

That beach was blocked off with barbed wire,
To stay an enemy's advance,
And never seemed the same again,
The child grew up.

Pollution now upon that beach,
That quiet, empty, evening beach,
A danger to a stooping child,
Peering in a rock pool.

Jean Frost

My Picture

Notes

I am 42 years old, married to
Stewart for 23 years and have
two grown up daughters,
Tracy aged 22 years and Alison aged 18 years. I live in
Newcastle-under-Lyme and
am a qualified NNEB.

I have, to date, had three poems published, entitled *Love,
The Crown Jewels?* and *The
Struggle.* Writing children's
stories and various types of
poetry has always been my
main hobby. I started writing
poetry when I was about ten
years old, mainly for my
friends to give to boys they
liked at school. Once I have a
title for a poem, I can usually
finish it within the hour. I
can write a poem any time,
any place, anywhere, I love
doing it so much.

I work in a nursery school
and am constantly amazed at
young children's vivid imaginations. My poem was based
on the imaginations of all
young children especially my
own two daughters when
they were young.

*Therefore, I dedicate this
poem to Tracy and Alison and
my great-niece, Caer, a very
imaginative five year old.*

The picture on my bedroom wall!
When I'm in bed it looks so small,
But when I stand upon my chair
And gaze at all the things in there,
A wondrous land my eyes can see,
A land that's meant for only me.
From in my bed, the pictures plain.
Some trees and flowers by a lane.
The lane it stretches far away
Towards a field that's filled with hay
But when upon my chair I stand
And look into that wonderland
Two little rabbits, behind a tree,
Hop out, to say *hello* to me.
And on the lane a snail crawls by,
And in the sky, a blackbird flies.
And if I'm quiet, as quiet as can be,
A mother mouse will wave to me,
She's in a bush, behind a door,
With babies, one, two, three and four.
The scarecrow, in the field of yellow,
Looks like such a jolly fellow.
He tips his hat and winks his eye
Whenever he sees me close by.
Into my picture I'd love to go
To visit friends and say *hello.*
But I'm too big and my pictures' small,
I wouldn't fit in there at all.
So I stand upon my chair
And chat to all my friends in there.
My picture friends living happily,
That only I can really see.

L J Barlow

Notes

I am 65, retired, live in York and have four grown up children.

I've had a poem published in Voices on the Wind, published by The International Society of Poets, and received the Editor's Choice award.

I am a spiritualist and for the last two years, I have received poems from Spirit, to date, 150. I am also a spiritual healer. I enjoy printing and making up my own poetry books to give to friends and family.

My Best Friend

Soft brown eyes gaze up into yours,
A paw gently touches your knee,
He knows you need comfort and that you are sad,
As if into your heart he can see.

How trusting they are, our animal friends,
Never judging or turning away,
They listen to all our stories of woe,
And you know that's as far as they stray.

They try so hard to give us support,
And to show that they really do care,
So show them some love and give them a chance,
And your troubles they really will share.

Joyce Woods

Notes

I was born in Edinburgh in 1954, moved to Wales in 1994, where I met and married a Welshman.

I became interested in writing because of my father, John Laing, as it was his hobby to write. About fourteen years ago, I started to write myself; besides poetry, I write children's and adult stories.

The inspiration came from my dog Bruno, who I had to put to sleep after having him for ten years. This is only the second poem I've had published.

I also enjoy reading and music. As I've only written in the past for my own enjoyment, I have only recently started to send in work, to the Cardiff Poetry Competition for example; on that occasion I was not successful, but I will try again.

I would like to dedicate this poem to my husband Alan, for his support and encouragement.

My Lost Love

I think of things before me,
My dearest partner's gone,
My life, work and pastimes,
With the birds he's flown.
We used to walk together,
We would also run and play,
What will I do without him?
Now he's gone away.

The days we spent together,
Then cuddle up in bed,
I'd talk for hours and hours,
He listened to what I said.
He'd then turn round and kiss me,
Of that I could depend.
He's my life, my friend and hero
Right to the very end.

I look at all his pictures
My memory lingers on,
To the things we did together
From the moment he was born.
I loved my little soldier
But had to say goodbye.
My heart was really breaking
I tried so not to cry.

I put him on the table
And held his little head.
Slowly I lowered him down
I knew that he was dead.
I went home to a lonely house
I can't control my tears,
And who can really blame me,
I'd had him all these years.

While in my bed at night-time,
I turn to him and say,
I will love you till forever
And every passing day.
I never will forget you
The pain I will endure.
'Cause dogs do have a heaven,
Of this I can be sure.

Margaret E Davies

Notes

I am Verona Coppack, 61 years old, married to Colin for almost 40 years and living in Connah's Quay, Flintshire. I am a grandmother to two little girls aged five years and two years. I am also a retired school librarian/media resources officer.

I have written poetry all of my life and have had two poems published. My first real success was first prize at the school Eisteddfod at Holywell Grammar School aged 11 years.

My hobbies include: writing poetry, painting (specialising in animal portraits), photography and my grandchildren.

I have also written a children's story in verse called *Willie the Welsh Dragon* which I am hoping will be published one day.

This poem is dedicated to all the young soldiers who have lost their lives in Northern Ireland over the years, and their families.

A Mother's Lament

So tall and so handsome, so smart and so straight,
As he walked down the path, as he went through the gate,
'See you soon, Mum,' he called as he waved me goodbye,
And the sight of him going brought a tear to my eye.

He was off to a war he did not understand,
Between civilised people in a green, pleasant land,
Oh why then, oh why did my son have to go,
Where he knew not his friend, and he knew not his foe?

His letters they told me of anguish and strife,
And as I read through them I feared for his life,
A life I had cherished from the day he was born -
A life that was ended on that cold, winter's morn!

So tall and so handsome, so smart and so straight,
Once he walked down the path, once he went through the gate,
Now they lay him to rest, one more victim of war,
'Goodbye son,' I whisper, 'I'll see you no more!'

Verona M Coppack

Notes

I am Barbara Hartshorn aged 58 years, my maiden name being Symons. I lived in Holsworthy, Devon and attended Holsworthy Secondary Modern School. I now live in Nuneaton, Warwickshire with my husband Geoffrey.

I now have four poems published which include: *1945, Glories of Devon, My Sister* and *Memories*.

Glories of Devon

Devon where the primrose grows
Devon where the water flows
River Tamer cool and clean
Otters playing by the stream.

Devon where you bend the rules
Devon with its lovely hills
Teddy pasty what a dream
Finishing - with scones and cream.

Golden beaches, oh so clean,
What it is to sit and dream
Memories - no longer bold,
Does this mean - I'm getting old.

Barbara Hartshorn

Memories

When I think of days gone by,
And memories of yesteryears.
The joys and sorrows that we shared
And the sadness of the tears,
Tears that fell with parting
When you went away,
Tears that lie, and stay smarting
In my heart all day.
Through the tears, there comes a light
A ray of sunshine, shining bright.
A thought to keep us all alert
And onward grows the night
For in the morning joy there'll be.
When we meet once more
Be it here at home, or far away
On some distant shore
We'll smile and say 'hello again,'
Joy will follow pain,
And who knows, perhaps, maybe
We'll never part again.

D B Rudge

Vanity

She was just an ordinary housewife
And one day when feelings pathetic
She took all her savings
She had made from her slavings
To a surgeon to have a cosmetic
He had her face lifted
Her mouth and nose shifted
He gave her a much firmer bust
He whispered my dear
You have such a large rear
A few pounds off is really a must
When she got back to her house
It was as quiet as a mouse
Her husband looked up in dismay
The kids cried if we're good
Wash windows, chop wood
Can we have our old mum back one day
So ladies when you feel down
And your face wears a frown
Find a salon that's really palatial
Just sit there in a chair
Let them mess with your hair
Have a manicure, a massage and a facial
Now don't start to get pensive
And think it's expensive
For this treatment will not go too far
To your husband and kids
You're worth millions of quids
'Cos they love you
Just the way that you are.

George Kaye

The Brook and I

Notes

I have been writing poetry for many years which I find relaxing and uplifting in thoughts. For only good thoughts attend poetry. In the first instance my penfriend sent several of my poems to Life Magazine who published them. I have a number in several various books also. My kind of poetry is not deep or clever, just simple and easy to understand. My favourite subjects are pertaining to nature, that is, flowers, trees, rivers, lakes and streams and of the seasons. Nature naturally, we are surrounded by it, and so on I go. I am 80 plus and still writing.

In the past I have also written many children's rhymes long before the days of Star Trek, Star Wars, Action Man and Power Rangers, enough for a book. I then cherished the hope that one day they would have been colourfully illustrated.

I have been a widow for 18 years and have three children, five grandchildren and eight great-grandchildren.

I love to wander by the brook
There to find a shady nook
Where to browse my favourite book
And sit me down to rest.
The ripple of the flowing stream
Caught in the sunlight's golden gleam
While I just sit, muse and dream
Of what I might have been.
A hazy sky lazy am I,
I care not how the time goes by,
The whispering grass and murmuring breeze
Whistling birds up in the trees
All these things do me please
I'll forget them never.
When I am older and I have grown bolder
I will build me a house on the hill
And everyday I will come this way
To wander here at will.
By the gentle brook and shady nook
Where all the world is still.

F M Rothwell

Notes

My age is 72, I have been a widow for eighteen years and have experienced lots of loneliness.

I have spent many hours writing poems, but have now had one printed. It has probably been a kind of release for me whilst lacking the normal conversation.

Untitled

The trees are so bare, and the wind blows cold
Oh! For that life without care, as we gradually grow old.
It's so hard and so lonely, when we sit here and stare,
At the winter scene only, aching for someone to care.
For spring to enter our lives once more,
For that friendship that means so much.
Our hearts are hurt to the core
For the true hand with the gentle touch.

W Pollard

A Passing

Notes

I am Edna Wilcox and am 76
years old. I have been writing
for the past six years or so
and gain a lot of pleasure
from doing so.

I have written about 200 poems and have had about 10
published. One in a Samari-
tan magazine and one in a St
John magazine. I have also
had a few published in my
church magazine.

This poem was written after I
lost someone very dear to me.

I look now at your empty chair
And yet I see you sitting there.
So many memories through the years
I can recall them through my tears.
We've shared so many years it seems
We've shared our love, our hopes, our dreams
I did my best to help you through
When life became too tough for you.
Life is hard to understand
I tried to give a helping hand.
Sometimes I failed to let you know
That I just always loved you so.
Wherever you are I know you'll be
Waiting to meet up with me.
Your latter years were in confusion
And I am under no illusion
That births and deaths affect us all
Whether we rise or whether we fall
It seems we're here to help each other
To call all people sister or brother.
It seems a life we all must follow
To lead a life without the sorrow.

Edna Wilcox

The Bingo Hall

Notes

Like many of the contributors, I write of life around me, and of my life, as it is at 76 years old, my frustrations, hopes, fears and the problems of loneliness, which is not hard to do, as my family is very scattered and I have no phone. I have one daughter in America, one daughter on Anglesey, a daughter in Bridgend and my son who lives in Mid-Glamorgan.

I have had my poems, *Elin Mair*, which was written about my granddaughter, and *My Daughter Faraway*, published.

I write poems instead of scribbling on my walls, which I have done at times. My son, who is my landlord and a very kind and understanding son, just says 'We'll have to give mother some clean walls to write on, and do the others up a bit.'

Eager faces, full of hope,
They come in droves to have a go.
No time here to sit and mope,
No time here, to get to low.

Up on the rostrum goes the 'lad'
O' how his face shines, 'he's not so bad!'
A scuffle for pencils, 'Hang on, Steve'
Here are the numbers . . .
'This one's mine, I believe!'
No! O' please, number eight,
O' please let it be.
'House!' Shouts someone;
O' gee, it was nearly me.

Vera Markham

Alone

Notes

I am a widow, aged 59: my husband died 27th November 1995. I have one daughter, Elizabeth Oulsnam (39) son-in-law, Ian Oulsnam and three grandchildren: Rebecca (16), John (8) and Eleanor (5). I am the resident manager of Nicholson Court, which is a sheltered housing complex belonging to Housing 21.

I have two poems about to be published in two separate books: *My Love* (dedicated to my husband) in Quiet Moments and *Flowers of Spring* (dedicated to my eldest grandchild, Rebecca, when she was a little girl) in Jewels of the Imagination, both published by The International Library of Poetry, one out this month and one in April, 1997. I have had another poem, *My Derbyshire*, published in *Rhyme and Reason* by Poetry Today.

My hobbies are writing poetry, playing cards (whist and bridge), playing bowls (indoor and outdoor), cooking, etc.

I have been writing poetry for many years, on and off. Inspiration to write comes suddenly; I may be driving the car or cooking a meal when I suddenly get an idea for a poem. I can't rest till I write it down.

This poem is dedicated to my husband, John Hollis, my lovely John.

You have gone to your rest, my darling
Your sweet face no more shall I see
I'll grow old on my own without you
Though I thought forever we'd be.
I can't follow where you've gone, my darling
You have left me alone and forlorn
Seems to me for this I've been waiting
Since the very day I was born
They placed you under soft earth, my darling
No more will you roam the green vales,
But lie in peace in the sunshine
With the wind whispering over the hills
I'll try my best without you, my darling
As winter creeps into my years
And think of you always in sunshine
As I wipe away all of my tears.

Elsie Hollis

Rover

Notes

This is my second poem to be published having previously had one published in your book *Rhyme and Reason*. I am 49 years old, unemployed and live alone.

Much of the poetry I see published is obviously designed to appeal to a very select few. It is refreshing to see that this is not always the case.

There was a young lady from Dover
Who mourned the loss of her dog Rover.
She was very fed up
At the loss of her pup.
An automobile ran it over.

Boyfriend said, 'Why not get another?
You could get some dosh from your mother?
You'd call it Rover too?
Sort of Rover Mark Two?
Keep it from the road? Then no bother!

So they went out and bought another
With cash they had had from her mother.
It ate rather a lot
But she cared not a jot,
So taken was she with new Rover!

R Edwards

Notes

My name is Isobel Crumley, I am 74 years old, married and have two sons, five grandchildren and one great-grandchild. I have been partially sighted since 1944 when I was caught up in a V2 rocket raid, which badly damaged my eyesight.

I have had ten poems published, mostly in books, also some in the local paper and talking newspaper. My hobby is writing poetry which my husband prints out for me, so they are readable from my bad handwriting.

I started writing poetry on the fiftieth anniversary of the end of the Second World War, which is what inspired me to write about my experiences. I have written many poems about my early life in Dunstable. I also write about local occasions, and personal poems for weddings, birthdays and happy or sad events.

A Pensioner's Thoughts

Today I did my shopping in
Our local super store,
And wondered how the younger folk
Could ever say they're poor.

I saw their filled up trolleys,
With things I'd love to buy,
But counting out my pension small,
I felt that I could cry.

When I was young we had to make
A meal from nothing much,
There were no pre-packed dinners then,
No cut sliced bread as such.

Fancy cakes were for the rich,
Our own we had to make,
If we'd no money for dried fruit,
Plain cakes were all we'd bake.

Faggots and peas, or fish and ships,
Some shops cooked those to eat,
But when you earned two pound a week,
They were a Saturday treat.

Our clothes were bought to last for years,
Our shoes till they wore out,
You couldn't buy the latest craze,
There was no cash about.

I'm glad the younger folk don't have
To scrimp and scrape like we
But how I wish the government
Would share things more evenly.

Isobel E Crumley

Notes

My name is Ruby Patricia Mary Hall, daughter of the late Thomas Camden MBE and Edith Camden. I am married to Frederick Hall and we will celebrate our Ruby Wedding on 20th April, 1997. I shall be 60 years old on 28th December, 1996. I have two children, Carole-Ann and Martin and two grandchildren, Benjamin and Timothy.

I live in a small village called Upton Snodbury situated in Worcestershire, where my husband and I have lived for 56 years. I am a housewife.

I was a former correspondent for Worcester Berrow's Journal and BBC Hereford and Worcester Radio.

My hobbies are reading, crosswords, walking, watching tennis on television, writing and spending time with my grandchildren.

I have written one story, 40 poems, seven of which have been accepted for publication. *Depression* was written after suffering clinical depression and father's death I started writing three years ago. I find it relaxing. My proudest and most memorable occasion was going to the Palace to see my father being presented with his MBE by The Queen. I now have the medal.

Depression

Depression is an illness we cannot see,
What we don't want is sympathy
But support, understanding and a listening ear
To which we can relate our fear.
For it is in a deep dark hole we are,
To look above we see no star,
Outside the world still carries on,
To us it has just gone simply wrong.
But fight we must to climb each rung,
Then our life has just begun.
The step's are hard, we falter back.
Once again we must retrace our track.
We try so hard, our minds to put right,
But everyday we have to fight,
One day our path goes the right way
And we have a better day.
Our life at last is going well,
On the past we must not dwell.

Ruby P M Hall

Notes

I am a forty one year old housewife, happily married to my wonderful husband, Peter. I have six children and live in Wales. My hobbies include animals and writing.

I have always wanted to write since I was eleven. One poem in particular, called *Land o' Spirits*, won an Editor's Choice award from The International Society of Poets and with whom I am proud to be a distinguished member. I was first inspired to write poetry after spending three months in Australia. I started writing in 1995, and I have had a number of poems published in various books. The inspiration for this poem, *Night Breed*, came from within; being afraid of the dark as a child, I realised to believe in the Lord brought me through each night until the morning light.

Today I dedicate this poem to my wonderful parents, Gertrude and Clifford Jones (deceased), who I know are with me each night and day and without them today would not be possible.

Night Breed

The rattle of chains
and shadows of night
there's ghostly goings on
when no one's in sight.

In the dead of night
the moans and wails,
from the church yard
tell a ghostly tale.

From midnight to dawn
they wander around,
all those ghostly spirits
coming from the ground.

When morning falls
the spirits disappear,
then no one knows
or has anything to fear.

So don't be afraid
of the dark night,
cause the Lord is with us
until the morning light.

R Maskill

Untitled

The roses blossom
In full bloom
And all around there is no gloom
The sun shine's down
Upon the ground
The birds are singing
What a sweet sound
The butterflies flutter
And clutter the trees
And everything sways
In the warm country breeze
The bees keep busy
Making some honey
Oh, what a nice day
And we've got plenty of money.

Patricia McNulty

Dollie's Nature Lesson

Notes

I remarried six years ago, leaving Bournemouth to live in Cambridgeshire. I am a 72 year old retired lady who uses poetry instead of a conventional diary.

With encouragement from husband, Geoffrey, I have published a collection of my own verse. I have had 100 plus poems accepted by Forward Press and have just self-published *A Village Hymnal* to which my husband has written the music. I also have had a runner-up prize in The Scottish Poets, Robert Burns contest, two editor's choice certificates and one poem professionally read on tape entitled *The Joy of Poetry*.

I have had four works accepted by International Society of Poetry (US) and one by The Poetry Guild. My second collection is now being published.

Little girl sat on the bank, Doll held in her arm,
Sun was shining overhead, all was soft and warm.
Puffy clouds, so white, above the dark green trees.
Wonders there in colours gay, for everyone to see.
When the water rippled, small child blew a kiss,
Said, 'see that Dolly, movement was made by fish
Swimming in that water, on which folk will boats sail.
Look, there is heron paddling, strong, though legs look frail.
Yesterday when near here a *crowd of frogs we saw,*
If we are *very lucky* today we may see more.
Across the fields behind us many rabbits play,
You'll see those bob-tailed bunnies happy in own way.
Bird life is stupendous, that is a real big word
It means they are the finest fowl, you will have seen and heard.
Feathers all colours, some bright, some very drab,
All of them sing sweetly, so you know they are glad.
Dad says Mister Badger has built his set nearby.
It's very hard to spot him, for that you need keen eye.
Sometimes we pick wild mushrooms though careful we must be,
Make certain they aren't toadstools. Those make one ill you see.
Look there is bright kingfisher, as well as him on high,
Are many flying insects, some like that big crane fly.
See coming up the river are some big snowy swan,
So much we have to look at, the time goes rushing on.
We must go home now Dolly, but we will patient wait,
And both return tomorrow, again to cogitate,
On Mother Nature's wonders, abundant every where,
All this for us to cherish, with special loving care.'

Barbara Goode

Cats in the House

Notes

I was born in Bushy, Hertfordshire 1st July 1942; married, gave up the theatre, had three children and have nine grandchildren. I now live in Berkhamsted, Hertfordshire.

I started writing poetry at school, but went on to do other things. I tried again in March 1996, and was published in November of this year. I have also had my poem put onto audio tape. I can't stop scribbling now. I also paint, play golf and swim.

I get my inspiration from the family and things that go on around me. This poem came to mind because of a friend called Caroline Baylis, who has two daffy cats like mine.

I have a cat, no! I have two,
Ming Ming and Ching Ching are what they're called,
If I call them by name,
Not a meow or purr is ever heard.
With a whistle, they are in like a shot.
One is male all black and sleek,
The other is fluffy and tabby but small.
She loves to eat and sleep, a lot.
But drop a pin, she will jump with fright.
She chases butterflies and flies through the air.
He bounds around, all over the place.
Chases his shadow and then his sister,
When she's quietly fallen asleep.
He watches and waits for her to stir
Up he jumps with a pounce at her,
She struggles to free herself, away from him.
Then off they go screeching around the house.
A biff and bat he lays her flat,
I whistle to them that breakfast is set,
She's like a bat out of hell and leaves him flat.

Diane E Complin

A Contented Fan

Notes

Patsy Coll was born Patricia Jackson, in Halifax, Yorkshire, in the 1930's, to a working-class background; the eldest of four children. She moved around the country through her first husband's employment, living in Leicestershire, London and the South East, and now lives in Lancashire. She has two daughters and three grandchildren from her first marriage.

Studying at evening classes she gained her O and A levels in English and French, plus secretarial qualifications. She retired early through ill-health, and started writing poetry and being quite successful, with most poems submitted being published in various anthologies.

Inspiration comes from personal experiences, emotions, nature and religious faith.

Dedicated to my husband, daughters and grandchildren.

I'll never enjoy your fame or fortune
For I can't entertain with song and dance
But, whilst you are adored by thousands of fans
I'm loved as a wife, a mum and a nan!
You've seen the world and the world has seen you
You've been welcomed in the finest of places
You've been courted by the rich and the grand
But I wouldn't swap my life for your life
For I'm loved as a mum, a nan and a wife!

Although I respect and greatly admire you
You can make my fantasies spring into life
As you take me into a magical space
Away from the humdrum and common place
When we two come to the end of our lives
You'll probably have all of your loyal fans
You'll surely have all that money can buy
Still I wouldn't swap my life for your life
I'll be loved as a nan, a mum and a wife!

Patsy Coll

Notes

I am a 64 year old retired officer for the elderly; my husband and I still live in sheltered housing where I worked for twenty seven years. We have three children and five grandchildren.

I had a poem, called *Purdie*, printed in the Mercury in 1979. Recently, I sent some work to Yours magazine, to be judged next spring. Because I have a thing about 'selling' my feelings, none of my work has been awarded, as such.

My hobbies are: writing, crosswords, piano and collecting Buddhas.

I wrote my first poem at school, 49 years ago and found I had a flair for it. The human race is my inspiration; I only write about feelings and get great pleasure from doing so. Ninety percent of my poems are written at night.

I would like to dedicate this poem to my granddaughter Carly Ives, who inspired me when she was a little girl dressing up in my net curtains.

Our Queen

Little girl's dream of being, a princess one day,
Dress up in their mother's clothes, 'let's pretend they say,'
For one little girl, it came true, her mother was a Queen,
They called her Elizabeth, she didn't have to dream,
Her father was our King George, a son he would prefer,
But when Elizabeth was born, he grew very fond of her,
She became his heir to the throne, her fate already planned,
The King knew she would rule well, his great and glorious land,
Then came the sad news, Liz had lost her dear dad,
Royals and their subjects, were all weepy and sad,
Then came the Coronation, Elizabeth became our Queen,
The whole ceremony was spectacular, the finest ever seen,
Forty years now, she has reigned over you and me,
Congratulations, Majesty on your anniversary.

Dixie White

The Father

Notes

I am Eileen Whiting, 57 years old, married with two children. I have a son, (31) and a daughter, (35) and two grandchildren aged 12 years and 14 years.

I have been writing poetry for one year and everyday things are special to me. Inspiration comes from my life when I was younger and now as I am more mature.

My hobbies are decorating, knitting and gardening.

This poem is quite simply about all fathers who work so hard.

A father's life
Is never planned.
He walks through life
Feeling grand
He works so hard
Hours on end
Earning money for the family to spend
But everything to him
Is worthwhile.
To come home to a loving smile.

E Whiting

A Happy Awakening

My eyes are heavy,
they yearn for sleep
I turn and switch out the light
plump up the pillows
pull the covers up high
and settle down for the night.
A welcomed calm
seeps through my body
easing every muscle, every bone
just as sleep
descends upon me
I hear the ringing of the phone.
The shrill tones
jump - start my mind
my hand reaches out for the receiver
'Hello' I mutter
and listen on -
nothing but a heavy breather.
Fear not, a crackle
the line is weak
a babbling voice comes and goes with the waves
it's faint, but familiar
then all is clear
it's the voice I've been longing to hear for days.
We chatter away
about what we've done
the time flies by, he says he has to go
but he'll be home soon
back on dry land
I only wish that day was tomorrow.

S Pugh

Water

Notes

I was a bookworm from a very early age, often being chastised by my mother for neglecting to do set chores. I particularly enjoyed strange sounding words, repeating them to myself over and over again; for example, 'Quinquireme of Nineveh from distant Ophir . . .'

Language and history were my two pet loves. These I revelled in when I became a mature-trained teacher. Now that I have retired I have the time to wallow in a bottomless ocean of literature and am inspired to try the art of poetry writing for myself.

Rain makes a wondrous, powerful sound
When it hurtles from clouds to bounce from the ground
Forming liquid temples that hang in space
Then drop with a 'plop' into a newborn lake,
A lake that slinks in ever-widening circles
Towards a crevice in the earth
Into which it drops with a joyful gurgle
Its body rushing after with infected mirth.

I love the gentle, mist-like rain
That lightly kisses the window pane,
Caresses the forms of flowers and fruit
With refreshing, sustaining life-giving juice.
It brightens the greens, sharpens the blues -
Makes vivid all colours of every hue.
Little creatures enjoy the newly-softened soil
And birds flutter moisture from their glistening wings.

P Reeves

Memories

Andrew John and Nicola Jane
Enjoyed their jaunts down Stoneybeck Lane.
Brother and sister, playmates and friends
Seldom apart until the day ends.

Two loveable rascals so full of fun,
Never seen walking when they could run!
Those two little heads with their shining hair,
Yet one was so dark and the other so fair.

His eyes were brown whilst hers were blue,
So unalike were the two of you.
You seemed so different in every way
But your bond grew closer day by day.

Nicola Jane and Andrew John
When they were naughty acted as one.
Neither was guilty or ever to blame,
Two innocent faces - always the same!

Oh Nicola Jane and Andrew John
Dear little pals where has the time gone?
I go still for walks down Stoneybeck Lane,
But without Andrew John and Nicola Jane.

Now they are grown and live apart,
Their lives have changed but not their hearts.
Brother and sister dear friends they remain
Always Andrew John and Nicola Jane.

Judy M Fennell

Memories

Notes

I am 62 years old, married with three children and four grandchildren. I live in Cwmbran, Gwent.

My hobbies include: reading, piano playing and walking. I'm also a voluntary tutor in an Adult Literacy class.

I started writing poetry May 1996 and have written 17 poems so far. My published work to date includes: *Living Near a Wood* (International Society of Poets 1996) and *The Vagrant* (Spring 1997), *People* (Poetry in Print - Spring 1997).

I enjoy writing poetry about memories and deep feelings about life.

Memories, with age, become more dear,
And looking back allays the fear,
That comes in time to everyone,
When all life's tasks are nearly done.

Blowing out the birthday candles,
Wearing pretty coloured bangles;
Thoughts like that bring childhood back,
Make up for all the things one lacks.

Schools had forty children in a class,
Some worked hard and gained a pass,
Going on to higher learning,
Keeping life's ambitions burning.

Sunday was a day of rest,
Maybe kids became a pest.
They had to go to Sunday School,
To keep dad's temper down real cool.

When I think of times gone past,
I do regret they cannot last.
One must look forward every day
To keep sad thoughts and fears at bay.

Audrey Donoghue

The Whitehall Warbler

Notes

Colin Thomas Guile, a native of Bridgend, Glamorgan, graduated at the University of Wales, Aberystwyth. Before his appointment as an advisory entomologist in the Ministry of Agriculture, Fisheries and Food, he served for two years as a hygienist in the RAF in the UK and Middle-East.

He aspired to writing poetry in early boyhood to cheer his ailing grandmother, reviving the interest after retiring from his profession.

His outlet is generally light-hearted rhyme for the amusement of the reader or audiences at social functions and relate to humorous incidents from his past or day to day happenings.

Other interests include: writing memoirs, wine-making and judging, country rambling, DIY, listening to light and classical music, local history and long distance swimming.

The Whitehall Warbler is a wily bird,
A cocky dick is he,
And when he's perched behind his desk
He slyly cries, 'tee, tee.'

He's often short of things to do,
His lot is such an irk,
And when he's brooding in his nest
He sobs 'mo-werk, mo'werk.'

He always keeps his pecker up
When a flap is on, 'tis true,
But if he fails to catch his worm
He goes 'cuc-koo, cuc-koo.'

His eagle eye is ever sharp
When office chicks fly through,
And if they flutter their pretty wings
He whistles, 'coo-coo-coo.'

But cackling clerks just drive him wild,
With them he will not sit,
And should they fail to make the grade
He calls them, 'twit, twit, twit.'

His brother wags try hard to please
With strutting pose and wit
But he swiftly clips their wings
By snapping back, 'cheez-it.'

His feathers never ruffle up
When the boss hawk starts his rows,
And if asked what, why or wherefore,
He idly sighs, 'who knows?'

When day is done it's home to roost
And a chirpy hen to please,
To him she's not a dainty dish
But a 'bit of bread and cheese.'

C T Guile

Notes

My full name is Marie Patricia Garvey, born in Scarborough in 1944, married to Patrick for thirty three years with three children, Mark, Tricia and Penelope. I love amateur dramatics and poetry reading and have worked as an extra.

I deeply thank my family for giving me the inspiration to write poems about the experiences of my life.

A thought from Penelope: Freedom lies in front of a caterpillar after, living the life of a snail being born again as a butterfly, joyously flying from her cocoon jail.

Fatastic!

The weight just seems to pile on,
From where, I just don't know,
I'm eating far less food now,
You'd think the fat would go.

Shopping is a nightmare,
All the clothes are tight,
Looking in the mirror,
It's not a pretty sight.

The bulges are enormous,
No wonder people stare,
The situation's desperate,
What am I going to wear?

A cover-up is needed,
One to pull me through,
Something big and floppy;
A nice long blouse will do.

At last the bulges disappear,
This blouse has worked a treat,
My appearance is fantastic,
I look so smart and neat.

Ah yes, that's so much better,
It feels just right for me,
And now that problem's over,
I wonder what's for tea.

P Garvey

Valley of Love

Notes

I was born in a small village near Wrexham, in North Wales. After World War II I served in the Royal Navy as a medic. I continued in this profession for the rest of my working life, being employed by the Ministry of Defence. On my retirement, I settled in South Wales.

I have been writing poetry for a number of years and have written over 50 poems. It is only recently that I have started to submit them for publication, and I'm pleased to say that some are coming out in various books in the near future.

My inspiration was Dylan Thomas, and a great love of Wales.

The valley I loved, is no more,
Deserted workings, hollow core.
Pain blasted to careless ear,
Crimson river, silent fear.

Cattle graze where men had toiled,
The crooked place, where molten streamlets, boiled.
Falls that brought a roaring past,
Meander shallow, no longer fast.

The cottage row of ancient lull,
Hides the place of worship, full.
Flood-gates that no longer halt,
Frail posts and iron fault.

The place I loved has gone forever,
But happy thoughts will never sever.
In winter's grasp, or summer's shine,
In all but flesh, you're ever mine.

Kenn Evans

13th March 1996

Notes

This is dedicated to my friends Kirsty, Karyn, Leah and Alison for all their love and patience over the years, and also for my mum for her continued support, encouragement and guidance throughout my life.

Dunblane - where were you God?
Those children so needlessly killed.
Did you stop it? - No
I wish you had been there,
I wish you had seen,
Did you sleep on that day?
All of these dreams fly through my mind.
You were there, you saw it,
You shared our nations pain.
Yet you gave us free will and you've no right to intervene.
Free will - what is this?
The right to choose
The right to know
The right to kill and pain?
And you must stand and see this happen,
Watch while evil takes its toll.
No help can be given - you simply
Heal our wounded souls.

Lorna Speirs

Tree

Notes

I live in a small village in Ayrshire, Scotland.

My hobbies are breeding and showing English springer spaniels, country music and writing poems and short stories. At the moment I have six pen-pals in the USA. My favourite singer is John Denver, his music, songs stories and commitment to the *planet* inspires many of my poems. His music takes me to places I long to be. John's pride and joy is the *Plant It 2000* campaign and I dedicate this poem to him in respect of his love for our Mother Earth.

Without people like John our future would be a lost cause. Without trees there is no future.

Tree, how come you grow so tall?
When once you were so tiny, so small
You stand there so regal, so grand
Surveyors of all this land
Your branches reaching up to the sky
And make a welcome resting place
For birds, as they fly
Soaring through space
You wear your coat of many shades
Casting each as the colours fade,
You command, no demand
The skill of the artist's hand
And the talent of the poet's pen
In return for all your beauty, you are ravaged by us, by men
We cut you down to fill our needs
The unsatisfying passion of man and his greed,
What will we do, when it's too late?
You'll be gone, what then our fate?

Cathie Mullen

Notes

I am 65 years old and live in
Aylesbury. I am happily
married (for the third time
nearly three years ago!).

I haven't written for many,
many years (when I really
only dabbled). Like so many
retired people, I have more
time to reflect and find writing, particularly poetry, very
therapeutic. Different occasions, situations, emotions,
relationships, etc, prompt me
to write.

Although not wealthy, we
have a happy, full but simple
life - entertaining friends,
dancing (tea!), gardening,
cooking and seeing grand-
children.

I have experienced many
traumas in life - some my
fault, some not - and happily,
I am now able to take stock
and count my blessings.

*This poem is dedicated to my
granddaughter, Lisa Pruden,
born 12th December 1981.*

A Grandmother's Love

Nearly fifteen now,
How quickly the years have flown.
It seems like only yesterday
My first grandchild was born.

'A baby girl' her Daddy says -
Music to my ears.
I whispered 'Thank you Lord' -
An answer to my prayers.

For always, always I had hoped
A daughter I would bear,
But I was blessed with two fine sons
And I thanked the Lord for those.

A granddaughter then - a gift indeed,
That bright December morn.
I loved her then,
I love her now
I shall until I die.
Those big brown eyes will
Dance for me
And plead to me
And cry.
And Granny will forever be her slave.

Joan Croker

The Chase

Notes

I am a housewife, aged 69,
married with four children
and eleven grandchildren. I
reside in Romsey, Hampshire,
a small market town on the
edge of the New Forest.

I started writing poetry
about twenty years ago, for
friends who wanted some-
thing to commemorate a
certain event (weddings, re-
tirements, birthdays, etc). To
get inspiration for my poems
the subject has to grip my
imagination.

My hobbies are reading and
crosswords.

I heard the screech, and I heard the squawk
Of the chicken and geese late at night.
'Old fox is about,' I said to the wife
I'll catch him and kill him if it takes all my life
So I pulled on my trousers and buckled my belt
Took my cap from the hook, and went off full pelt
With gun in my hand and dog by my side
I went out of the door and up to the ride.
The blighter lay low, but I was in no hurry
I just stood there quiet, without any worry
When out of a hole in the bank I did spy
A vixen with cubs, and I gave a big sigh.
What a terrible decision I had to make
Should I let her live, for those little cubs sake
No, I'll shoot, so I aimed my gun well
But I dropped it again as they ran down the dell
I followed on foot as fast as I could
But once again they hid in the wood,
The leaves gave a rustle, the twigs I heard snap
I stumbled and slipped, and off fell my cap
I scratched at my head, swore under my breath
As I looked to the right, and I looked to the left.
That wily old vixen was off once again
Under the trees, and off down the lane
I took a short cut through the copse to the hill
And there I lay on the ground very still
She came into view, cubs following behind
They stopped to eat rabbit, and I watched as they dined,
My heart then got the better of me, as I watched this picture and I could see
The killing of the vixen was not for me
So I turned on my heel, and started for home,
When out rang a shot, a howl and a cry
Some other man had been braver than I.
I looked at the scene, the vixen lay dead
The cubs were nuzzling and licking her head,
I felt really sick, that man was so cruel
He didn't believe in letting the animals rule.

Nora M Brown

Notes

I am retired and started writing children's stories when my daughter was small. I have had one published.

I also wrote a nativity play and produced it in our church. I started writing poems when I was ill in hospital and watched the nurses hurrying about the ward, and wrote two poems before I came home.

I saw a beautiful rainbow over the valley and remembered a childhood story of a crock of gold, so this poem was the result.

At the End of the Rainbow

At the end of the rainbow shall I find -
A crock of gold? But I should not mind -
If at the end of the rainbow I should find
True happiness, that illusive kind.

True happiness, that gift from *God* to man
Only few really know it, few really can -
Offer love true and unselfish, ready to ban -
Hate, greed and jealousy, that gift from *Devil* to man.

Stella Askew

Start of a Day

Notes

My name is Aln Hall and I live in the north-east of England, once a thriving shipbuilding and coal mining area, now alas all gone.

I have been writing poetry since I was sixteen and I am now 43 years old. I have had two other poems published.

I enjoy walking and often take my book to write down anything that comes to me. I love music of all types and used to write songs with a partner. I have also written a couple of children's stories.

Just over there, the rooftops, the sun,
Just over there, the day has begun.
Is all the world asleep 'cept me
Am I the only one awake to see.

This marvel this rising, this planet so far.
From another galaxy it looks like a star.
Who else not from here could be seeing this sight
The birth of the day from the mother of night.

And then I awake as the milk float goes by
White puffy clouds in a pale blue grey sky
Flowers on the window-sill yellow and red
The sun kisses them, they all raise their heads.

I look, it's six thirty, the household stirs
And draws me away from writing this verse.
It's time to make coffee, toast and an egg
It's time to stop dreaming let's go shake a leg.

Aln Hall

The Rotunda

Notes

I was born in Liverpool March 7th, 1934, as Anne Ferguson and married Lewis Farrugia in 1981.

The pen name, Comer, is after my maternal great-grandmother's maiden name.

The Rotunda was a local theatre I remember
as a child, which stood on the main Scotland road
of old Merseyside, often I was taken there
much to my delight, even though it meant
climbing seemingly endless steps to reach
the Gods on high.

But alas in a Jerry air-raid
one night, it was razed straight
down to the ground, no more
in sight, leaving saddened
regulars with tears in their
eyes at the blight.

Sarah Comer

Pebbles

Different shapes I see
When looking at the pebbles by the sea.
Some I turn into a dog
Some could be a fat bull-frog.
Shells into pictures I make
To give my friends for a keepsake.
Some into lamps are made
This can become quite a trade.
If one enjoys giving,
Or perhaps want to do this for a living,
Then pay a visit to the shore
You will find many things to adore.

Patricia M Farbrother

Dunblane

Notes

I am 49 years of age, married with two daughters, one of whom is married.

My hobbies include: gardening, cooking, theatre, music (piano) and poetry.

Poetry has been part of my life since young. I love writing, especially when I feel deeply about something.

The Dunblane tragedy was so very sad I just had to write down my feelings.

Dunblane you must be in so much pain
All because a man was insane
A sick and evil man was he,
Not meant to mix with society.
Dunblane your hearts must be broken in two
Those sweet innocent children taken from you.

Mothers and fathers, grandpa's and grans,
With tears in their eyes and trembling hands.
How your lives have been shattered
On that awful day when people nattered.
Each went about their day not knowing that.
A wicked man, a dirty rat.
Was entering their little school,
He was full of hate and had lost his cool,
He went berserk and fired his gun.
Those poor little children had nowhere to run.
Their teacher tried as she could to shield,
But he shot her as well it was like a battlefield.

What a waste of life, they were so small,
They never should have died, not at all.
Dunblane you need to be left in peace.
Get out press, onlookers, can't you cease.
Let the people cry their tears
Grieve their children of so few years,
Only those who have lost someone near
Can know the ache, can shed the tear,
Dunblane you will never forget, your village died that day.
Little folk going to school, to work, to laugh, to play.
No one would ever have thought it,
That evil was so near,
For if we thought that way.
Our lives would be in constant fear,
The community will survive for those children that are still alive.

Time will heal,
But we must appeal,
Ban guns,
Keep evil people under lock and key,
Oh! What a better world it would be,
Dunblane the nation weeps for you,
But no one knows what to do.

Carol Whitnall

Music Therapy

Notes

My name is Mary Scott and I was born in Eire in 1936. I am married and living in Glasgow and we have four grown up sons.

Music is my main hobby as I play keyboard, guitar and banjo but Country and Western/Irish are my favourite to listen to.

I taught for over thirty years and for the last eight years I was working with children with severe learning difficulties due to mental/physical impairments like blindness and deafness. I witnessed the tremendous enjoyment of these children but more important was the vast difference that music sessions made to their limited life-styles.

I love writing poetry and writing personalised poems for friends. I have written poetry for years and have had around fifty published.

My Daddy taught me to love music when I was very wee
He sang songs and he hummed tunes as I was sitting on his knee,
I sang to my own children too when I was putting them to bed
If I was really busy I'd put a wee tape on instead.

Children naturally love music and it makes them more aware
And helps with their vocabulary and they enjoy it anywhere,
That's why in nurseries and infant schools they get music every day
With action songs and games too so it's a natural form of play.

Music lessons are invaluable for children with special needs
As their physical or emotional problems mean that they all learn
at different speeds.
I remember one wee blind boy who insisted on *playing* the piano each day,
And a teenage Downs Syndrome girl who could communicate no other
way.

The music teacher is the favourite and most popular teacher in special
schools,
As everyone loves playing the instruments and she holds all these musical
tools.
Like . . . the piano and the xylophone, the chime bars and the drums,
So children learn to wait for their turn on the 'Ta Rum Ta Rum Ta Rums!'

Music Workshops are now commonplace and it's also used as therapy
For all kinds of emotional and physical problems it's wonderful you see . . .
In psychiatric and geriatric wards music sessions are *all the go!*
As it can stimulate the memory so bring back scenes of long ago.

So apart from the obvious enjoyment that music can so often give
It can be responsible for giving back confidence and restoring a reason to
live,

The therapeutic value is immense and rightly so
But of course it is expensive and requires a *lotta doh!*

Mary Anne Scott

Notes

Alison Margaret Dobell is 43 years of age, a widow and a serving Woman Police Officer with the Kent County Constabulary. She lives and works in Margate where she has been stationed for the last twenty years. Originally from Devizes in Wiltshire, Alison has been writing poetry since she was seven years old and had a book of poetry published in 1981, *Shades of You, Shades of Me.* She also writes stories, songs, and fan fiction. Alison has written a fantasy novel, *The War of the Winter Night,* which has yet to be offered for publication.

No Common Man is a tribute to all those people who struggle against the trials and tribulations of day to day human existence yet still retain their humanity and take the time to reach out to those around them less fortunate. It is a salute to the ordinary people who live their lives in an extra-ordinary way and is dedicated in particular to my father.

No Common Man

'My father is a common man
Salt of the earth, his wit demands
Worthy toil for his daily bread
To earn his respite and his bed.

No beggar's mummer - he defies
The ways of sloth or those of lies,
An honest man who understands
The gold of working with his hands.

Bright eyes bespeak his intellect
While humour lingers in every breath,
Whether spoken or in his smile
The merest look can so beguile

That even the most weary heart
Will lift enough to share his laugh;
And unthinking journey on
This treasure I was raised upon.

So think you not that I am poor
With treasure such as this in store:
The gold of laughter through the years
The silver wisdom that appears
To give content where others have none -
My father is no common man . . .

Alison M Dobell

Slumber

Notes

Inspired by my granddaughter.

She said, 'Nanna Nooie, please make me better'
I've got a headache and feel under the weather
The face in earnest, full of hope
'Please God, said I, 'Help me to cope.'

To ease the pain of my little patient
I used the potion, magic and ancient
Into my bosom, I cradled her there
A few kind words and loving care.

I stroked her head and eased her mind
And blessed the Lord for being kind
For after slumber, Lucy did flee
And said, 'Nanna Nooie, come play with me!'

Doreen Hough

My Restful Day

Notes

Roberta Lucius Clarke is a mother of two children, aged three and four years. She has written several poems about her hectic life with her two children.

They're poems with an insight into her busy life with the bairns and that there is never a dull moment.

Up at six, nothing to do?
Yes, I have, loads to do,
Now Toby's three and Georgie's two,
Stop! It's George, she's crying again,
She's out of bed 'Mum - ju-i-c-e.'
Run down the stairs to clear out the fires
Poke them and lay them, what are those cries?
'J-u-i-ce' she whines, 'What shall I do?'
Bring in the milk and pick up a shoe
Toby is up, breakfast to make,
I'll be ready in just a shake,
Feed them and change them and dress them today
In case the 'phone rings for teaching, it may!
Today, tomorrow or let's see when,
Eight-thirty ready to work just then,
But no, it's Toby's day for school,
No time to waste - coats - just two,
Ready to leave, we have to go
Cross the Tyne and follow the flow.
Toby's tired, Georgie's cross,
What's the problem, why the fuss?
'Where's teddy?' Oh, gosh no,
He's at home but we have to go
Off to school, no time to waste,
We're in a rush, quick, make haste.
Leg it back home, time to rest
No, not really, you must have guessed,
Hoovering, ironing, washing, oh no!
Cupboards are bare, have to go,
Dash through the supermarket at full speed
So I've something to cook, and ready to feed
The hungry bairns and hubby too,
Time's just flying, still more to do
Six o'clock bath and bed
Time for my shower, then rest my head.

Roberta Lucius-Clarke

Notes

I am middle-aged and live in a small village in Cambridgeshire, with my husband Michael and son Colin.

My hobbies: are gardening, painting, flower arranging and reading.

I have been writing poetry for approximately one year and have had four other poems published, *Reluctant Bride, Sooty, English Summers* and *Snookered.*

I was inspired to write *Life,* after I had been watching the news on television.

Life

Often, I have wondered,
What is life about?
I have lived for many years,
And still can't work it out.

This world's a mix, of good and bad,
Floods, disease, and droughts,
Misery, and happiness,
Faith, hope and doubts.

If we all work together,
Help the poor, the sick, and troubled,
Then *happiness,* will triumph,
And our blessings, surely doubled.

Pauline Markham